C000181407

Heaven on Earth

A Calendar of Divine Hotels Around the World

Credits & Acknowledgements

Many many thanks to all my family, friends and colleagues who have supported me with their enthusiasm and humour through this journey – and to the welcoming hoteliers and friendly fellow travellers, who enriched the whole experience. In particular, my heartfelt thanks go to my agents Sheila Ableman and Silke Bruenink; my editor Christine King; Adrian Huett, Carole McDonald, Lyn Davies and Julian Flanders at Butler and Tanner; my mother Anne Hurst and sisters Nikki Stocks and Lilla Hurst for all their family support; Ivana Znamenackova; Michael and Lulu Hart; Adrienne Eastwood; Louise Hounsell; Ugo Baccanello; Gloria Beyer; Helen Edwards; Mary Anne Denison-Pender; Bruce Roxburgh; Elaine Vaughan; Mandy Chambers; all at ZFL and Columbus; Rob Sherwood; Katherine Rumens; Air Canada; British Airways; and always to my husband Johnnie, for his endless support and love, without whom *Heaven on Earth* would never have got further than a dream.

None of the hotels in *Heaven on Earth* have paid a fee to be featured. Nor was the author at any stage under any obligation to include them. The final collection has been made from a selection of over 1,000 hotels.

The author would like to thank the following for providing photographs and for permission to reproduce copyright material. While every effort has been made to trace and acknowledge all copyright holders, we would like to apologise should there have been any errors or omissions.

All pictures supplied by hotels, resorts, tourist boards and author, except for the following:

Dhoni Mighili Sakis Papadopoulos/Impressions pp 90 & 91;
Hacienda San Rafael James Fletcher p92 & p102;
Hotel Ritz Turespaña pp117 & 121;
Orient Express Camps Wilderness Safaris p149
Quark Expeditions Martin Enckell p242 & 245, Tom Schandy p243, Roger Slade p246 , Galen Rowell p247;

Please be advised that some of the information contained will have changed since publication. The opinions expressed in this book are those of the author and do not represent the opinions of the publisher. The publisher shall not be liable for any deficiencies in quality, service, health or safety at any of the hotels. All complaints must be made directly to the hotel concerned. While the publisher has made every endeavour to ensure that the information contained in this publication is accurate, it will not be held liable for any expense, damage, loss, disappointment or inconvenience caused, in whole or part by reliance upon such information.

First published in 2004
© Sarah Siese and St Christopher's Publishing Ltd

Sarah Siese has asserted her right to be recognised as the author of this work

St Christopher's Publishing Ltd
PO Box 5346, Reading, Berkshire
RG7 2YN

ISBN 09547 93110 pb
ISBN 09547 93102 hb

All rights reserved. No part of this book may be reproduced in any form by any means without prior permission in writing from the publisher, except by a reviewer who may quote brief passages in a review

Design, layout, reprographics, printing and binding by Butler and Tanner Limited Frome and London

For Johnnie

Heaven on Earth is quite simply the most alluring travel book ever written –
Sarah's evocative descriptions will delight even the most discerning traveller.

Peter de Savaray
OWNER OF BOVEY CASTLE

Contents

Kids

Introduction

As long as I can remember, I've had a passion for travelling, which has taken me all around the world from Antarctica to Zululand, staying in everything from tents and boats to lodges and grand palaces. The question I'm most often asked is, 'What is your favourite place?' – rapidly followed by, 'What is the best hotel to stay in?' For me, the irresistible hotel is one that embodies the essence of its location, combining indigenous authenticity with individual flair and excellent personal service. My favourite hotels are those that meet these exacting standards, and *Heaven on Earth* is a collection of the crème de la crème. Some of them are well-known classics; others are little gems that hardly feature in magazines or brochures. All of them are worthy ambassadors for their countries, guaranteeing an authentic and unforgettable experience.

I know that finding the right holiday can often be an exasperating and arduous process, spending hours deciphering dozens of brochures, gambling which will live up to expectations. Most of us have only a few precious weeks a year to escape – which makes a reliable recommendation all the more valuable. In my quest for excellence, I have stayed at each of the following forty-five hotels (as well as hundreds of others), and can assure you that *Heaven on Earth* will help you discover the paradise of your dreams.

Because we generally choose our holidays around what time of year we want to go, followed by which type of activity or part of the world we want to explore, it made sense to divide this book into calendar chapters – each one depicting the very best month to visit, thus avoiding bad weather (guaranteed to ruin any holiday) but incorporating any unmissable cultural events.

Each chapter begins with a hotel in one of the world's most enchanting cities followed by at least two hotels located in areas of outstanding natural beauty. The Kids chapter contains three hotels that will keep both parents and children happy, during each of the main school holidays. No compromises have been made with adult creature comforts, while encompassing all the desires that will keep children blissfully content for days on end.

Heaven on Earth has been a labour of love to research and write, thanks to all the wonderful people I have met who give every day of their lives to making our holiday experiences memorable – for all the right reasons.

Where is your Heaven on Earth?

January

The Mount Nelson

Cape Town

Dominated by the scenic wonder of Table Mountain, Cape Town has it all: long, empty, white sandy beaches, exotic botanical gardens, ancient and contemporary culture, gastronomic excellence, world-class wine and heavenly shopping. And its natural setting is breath-takingly beautiful. At the very tip of the African continent, where the warm waters of the Indian Ocean meet the chill of the Atlantic, it was justly described by Sir Francis Drake as 'the fairest cape in the whole circumference of the earth'.

Lying at the foot of Table Mountain, but within reach of the buzzing hub of downtown, the Mount Nelson Hotel has been the key symbol of Cape hospitality since 1899. Affectionately known as the 'Nellie' by locals and regular patrons, this grand old lady has certainly seen some life over the years – and she's wearing well!

Originally opened to provide luxurious accommodation for passengers of the old Union and Castle shipping lines, the Nellie has lived her own tale of adventure, survival and endurance during the tumultuous events of South African – and world – history.

Reputed for her elegance, luxury and service, the colonial Nellie feels like a cocktail combination of London's Hurlingham, the Beverly Hills pink palace in Los Angeles and Nairobi's Maithaga Club. Resting in nine acres of mature landscaped grounds, the 'English' gardens are awash with the pastel colours and fragrance of roses, agapanthus, oleanders, honeysuckle and the curious *Brunfelsia pauciflora* – better known as the yesterday, today and tomorrow plant.

Most of the 201 rooms and suites are based in the elegant main residence. The remainder are found in four architecturally significant buildings along the driveway, itself graced with giant canary palm trees, and are linked by a series of paths and sheltered courtyards. All rooms enjoy views overlooking the magnificent gardens, with some facing the cloud-draped 'Tablecloth' Mountain.

One of the most charming annexes is the cream-walled Edwardian Helmsley Building; a national monument today and originally built as a synagogue. Each room is named after an illustrious vessel, and the walls are chock-a-block with photographs of grand liners and military battleships – a curiously apt link between its owners, Sea Containers, and its heritage.

Generously-sized suites in this wing have a refined country decor with chintzy fabrics and floral carpets in neutral cream and greens. Each suite benefits from a separate living and dining area, a walk-in dressing room and small kitchenette. The chestnut-brown marble bathrooms, liberally supplied with Ken Turner unguents, are well designed, incorporating a double vanity and separately enclosed loo and shower.

For George Bernard Shaw, who once remarked that 'There is no love sincerer than the love of food', Cape Town cuisine would be a gastronomic paradise. Locals evidently revel

Helmsley Wing. **The Chef's Table.** (opposite) **Planet Bar.**

in their abundant supply of fresh produce, and healthy eating is de rigueur across the Cape. Throughout the day the Nellie has a spoiling choice of dining options, encapsulating the new food and wine culture of the country. Breakfast is best taken al fresco on the calm lavender-edged terrace of the elegant Oasis Restaurant. Overlooking the pool and gardens, you can sit back and watch the entertainment from the resident ibis, Guinea fowl and squirrels. Lunch is a lavish Mediterranean buffet in the same location after which – if you can still move – a belt-busting tea is served in the commodious flower-filled conservatory and terrace.

Dinner at the chef's table in the Cape Colony kitchen is both an education and an entertaining novelty. Recently introduced by the renowned Stephen Templeton – a leader in the field of culinary innovation – it reflects the chef's and the hotel's confidence to allow up to ten diners to indulge themselves with a peek behind the scenes. Stephen enthuses that, 'Modern cuisine is not just about mixing different influences. It is more about an approach to food – the style of preparation, seasonality and freshness of ingredients.' He believes that food must express its personality by allowing its true flavour to emerge. The influences used to enhance the principal flavour are considerable but are never too overpowering or confusing.

He starts the menu with a shot glass of mango and chilli to awaken the taste buds. Then one of the dishes of the five-course extravaganza, such as an entrée of tuna pancetta, is prepared in front of you as a demonstration dish. All this against a back-drop of sous and commis chefs completing orders coming in from expectant diners in the Cape Colony Restaurant – and not a swearword to be heard all evening.

The Restaurant itself is the place for you if the heat and excitement of the kitchen are all too much – a serene oasis where the atmospheric centrepiece is an expansive trompe l'oeil landscape of Table Mountain and Devil's Peak. Regional gourmet delights such as smoked crocodile, Karoo lamb and ostrich fillets are typical of the fine dining choices, matched with the flavours of well-endowed wines from the local Stellenbosch and Constantia wineries.

A perfect siesta spot is on one of the thick-mattressed sun-loungers in a quiet corner of the luscious gardens by the main swimming pool, where you can enjoy one of the Cape's best views of Table Mountain without straining your neck. If you're feeling energetic, there's a well-equipped gymnasium and two pristine

(opposite) **Writing Room.** **Suite.**

floodlit tennis courts next to the drive. If not, indulge in a massage or treatment in the body care centre.

The last decade has proved to be one of the most challenging periods in the country's turbulent political history. Much of the hotel's success today is credited to the unfailing optimism of Swiss-born managing director Nick Seewer, who has steered the Nellie through by means of a passionate hands-on management style. In his unstinting concern for guest comfort he has slept in every one of the hotel's rooms – when vacated, he assures me – and is treasured as a benevolent father figure and mentor by staff and guests alike.

The hotel offers a huge range of excursions all within an hour's drive, that will surely tempt you out of the gates. The most popular sightseeing trip is perhaps the romantic cable car ride up Table Mountain at sunset. High above the roar of the city, you can gaze down at the panoramic view towards Cape Point and the jutting peaks known as the Twelve Apostles. As the fresh south-easterly breeze known as the 'Cape Doctor' brings in fresh sea air and blows away the old stale air, it

cascades over the mountain, refreshing walkers. It is hardly surprising that this spot is celebrated as one of the world's top ten places for marriage proposals!

Down below, the vibrant Victoria and Alfred waterfront has undergone a complete facelift over the last decade. It's been trans-formed from industrial dockland to the leisure heart of the city, buzzing with shops, restaurants, museums and an aquarium.

Wine-lovers shouldn't miss a tour of Stellenbosch, Paarl, Franschhoek and Constantia with their ubiquitous vineyards. Interestingly, today's grape cultivars are leaning towards fresher and lighter Sauvignon Blancs and spicy Gewürztraminers. Combining a trip with a delicious lunch in one of the stunning Dutch Cape homes such as Lars Maack's Buitenverwachtching – appropriately translated as 'beyond expectations' – makes for a truly heavenly experience.

Artists will be happy to know that Dr Shirley Sherwood, wife of the Chairman of Orient-Express Hotels, recognised for her world-renowned botanical art collection, has organ-ised a special course of botanical and flower

painting master classes in the hotel, with visits to nearby Kirstenbosch gardens.

The Nellie will always hold a little extra affection in my memories, as it was here that I watched and then toasted the triumphant English rugby team on that sunny November day in 2003. The chivalrous support from the native Springbok crowd in the champagne bar was a boon to every nail-biting England supporter who agonised throughout the match.

The Month
January is midsummer in Cape Town and brings with it long hot days and balmy evenings. The New Year starts with a parade through the city centre on 2 January (an informal public holiday) known as the Kaapse Klopse or Minstrels Carnival. There are dozens of food, wine and flower festivals throughout the summer, and the popular open-air Maynardville Shakespeare Season held in Maynardville Park. The Jazz Festival is held in the middle of the month down on the waterfront, which also sees the start of the Cape to Rio Yacht Race – all in all, a busy month with something to suit everyone.

The Datai

Langkawi

Langkawi consists of a group of ninety-nine tropical islands lying off the north-western peninsula of Malaysia. The main island is popularly known as Pulau Langkawi, and enjoys its intriguing heritage of ancient secrets and romantic legends of gigantic birds, fairy princesses, ogres and battles. It has a rich geological history dating back more than 500 million years and is blessed with beautiful beaches, warm emerald waters, dense virgin rainforest, caves (with stalactites and stalagmites) and characteristically shaped islets. The stunning lime-green paddy fields strike a contrast against the cool mountain mists.

Everywhere you are greeted with warm hospitality and friendly smiles from the local people. Winding rainforest roads often encounter roaming buffalo and are dotted with a multitude of small stands selling anything from banana fritters and cashew nuts to obscure local medicines. The island is a refreshing paradox of modern times where a tightly controlled tourism policy has left a rich culture intact – the two work harmoniously and thrive. Local people claim this to be the legacy of Mashuri, a pretty young maiden living some 200 years ago, who placed a curse on the island after being executed for a crime she did not commit. It would appear that Pulau Langkawi has risen from 'the seven generations that shall not prosper', and is emerging as an eminent twenty-first-century holiday setting.

Reminiscent of a modern-day Noah's Ark, the impressive Balinese-style architecture of the Datai makes an immediate impact. The open reception is dominated by two huge Trojan horses in front of a waterlily pond surrounded by the bar, beyond which the eye is drawn to the far-reaching views across to mainland Thailand. The accommodation leads from long open-air corridors, linking the fifty-four deluxe rooms and fourteen suites housed within this 'ark'. Hidden by the lofty canopy of the virgin tropical rainforest on the north-west tip of Langkawi, its secret whereabouts is perfectly camouflaged from human eyes.

The hotel has been skilfully located between the imposing Macincang Mountains and the Andaman Sea. To imaginative minds, the exposed buttress roots and jungle twines surrounding the property evoke a Tarzan habitat – the feel is very much of a treetop jungle safari. It was built in 1993, and its architect Kerry Hill chose sensitively, connecting a combination of Mayan walls, Malay roofs and Japanese screens. Today the Datai still takes pride in its eco-friendly ethos, ensuring that for every tree that has to be cut down, a new one is planted – guests are even encouraged to go and plant their own seeds down by the river.

The rooms have been decorated in tones and materials complementary to their forest surroundings. Polished wooden floors and furniture including a writing desk and two daybeds, cream walls and leaf-green blankets are stylish but simple. The *Datai Nature Guidebook* explains the cacophony of noise

Stylish suites.   Jungle canopy.

courtesy of Mother Nature outside the room, replacing the sounds of the CD player. The hip reading lights each side of the king-size bed are the finest and most practical to be found anywhere. Bathrooms resonate with the natural theme, using indigenous Langkawi marble on the twin vanities, shower and bath, and the warm red balau surround is decorated with fresh orchids. Simple but chic.

The small balcony gives you a simply breathtaking view overlooking the treetops, glimpsing the shadows of the mountains on mainland Thailand and the deep blue waters of Datai Bay. Down below, a meandering path leading towards the beach links forty-four villas secluded by the dense rainforest canopy. It's hard to believe that they are only steps away from the open sea. While much darker than the 'ark' rooms, the larger villas do enjoy the benefits of their own private deck with sun lounges (some with pools) and an elevated dining veranda.

'Manadara' is a word synonymous with excellence in the world of spas. The idyllic location of the luxurious spa villas, deep under the jungle canopy next to an ambling stream, must be a feng-shui dream. The Asian treatments have been given an innovative interpretation and the signature treatment, 'the Manadara Massage', is the ultimate pamper – two spa therapists working simultaneously up and down the body combining the five styles of Thai, Swedish and Balinese massage, Shiatsu, and Hawaiian Lomi Lomi. This is not only the best spa on the island but one of the best in the world.

Breakfast is an elegant affair taken in the formal dining room. The colourful spread is displayed along the full length of the back wall, leaving guests to gaze out at the forest canopy and waters down below. Service is exemplary, if a little too formal at times. There are three choices for dining; the most dramatic and authentic is the Pavilion Restaurant, specialising in delicious Thai fusion cuisine. It's built on huge stilts, elevating the balcony so diners overlook the rainforest. Malaysian and western specialities are served in the more formal Dining Room and the best option for lunch is the alfresco Beach Club. On special occasions such as Valentine's Day, international celebrity chefs are invited to

come and serve their distinctive specialities to guests seated on chairs draped in gold around the candle-lit swimming pool.

The most popular of the array of leisure activities is golf at the adjacent eighteen-hole championship course, nominated as the third best in south-east Asia. It is particularly pleasant in late afternoon when the cool tangy breezes sweep across the fairways. An assortment of windsurfing boards and sailing boats are to be found down on the beach, or you can

Main swimming pool.   Irshad.   (opposite) **Lush tropical setting.**

simply laze languorously by one of the swimming pools. Sipping cocktails and watching the sunset from the sixty-year-old motor yacht *Kanangra* is a real treat. The beautiful sixty-foot yacht cruises at a steady eight knots towards the Tarutao Island in Thailand and is a spectacular way to finish any day. A small word of caution: only attempt the trip to the Pulau Payar Marine Park on a privately chartered yacht, or you'll be caught up in a mass cattle-herding experience from which it will take the rest of the week to recover.

Maybe it is the design of the hotel, or perhaps it is because it is more like a club than a hotel experience, that the Datai has been garlanded by visitors with the weighty title of Best Hotel in the World! The eclectic mix of international clientele is certainly more friendly here than elsewhere, and conversation quickly germinates new friendships among strangers, many returning here on an annual basis. Old-timers welcome new blood with smiles and friendly banter as if to congratulate them for discovering the centre of their secret maze.

However, the main reason to visit this hotel is not for the pleasure of the design, the interesting clientele, unique setting, hedonistic spa, or epicurean cuisine. The Datai has to be experienced for one reason alone: Irshad, the hotel's very own naturalist. After years in the banking world, Irshad experienced snorkelling while on holiday and became enchanted by a whole new world. He ripped the tie from his neck, left his commercial success behind and began his life-long love affair with nature.

He excels at teaching others about the fascinating and fragile ecosystem in Langkawi. He raises his audience's awareness and maintains attention with amusing banking analogies: the Giant Fig's strangling effect on its victim is exposed as a 'hostile takeover bid'. Only David Attenborough matches his ability to arouse interest in the most common of species found along the roadside and normally taken for granted. He can hold a group spellbound for over half an hour looking at the abundance of life underneath one footprint.

This is a man at home in an environment most find alien and a little threatening. His encyclopaedic erudition and ability to translate complicated and what could be boring detail into captivating and unforgettable stories never fail to entertain and inform. The morning nature walks, rainforest by night and coastal mangrove or kayaking tours are all opportunities not to be missed. Returning home enriched with new knowledge about the various species of hornbills squawking overhead, abundant geckos, pink dolphins and white-bellied sea eagles is a more memorable souvenir than any meal, swim or massage. Be warned: after a trip with Irshad, you might just be ripping off your own tie!

Tanjung Rhu

Langkawi

Currently a little gem that hardly anyone knows about! The very few holiday brochures that feature Tanjung Rhu just don't do justice to this exquisite corner of the island. Set on the northern cape of Pulau Langkawi, the Tanjung Rhu is home to the island's most beautiful beach, as any local will testify. Spread over thirty acres, the resort is surrounded by an abundance of palms and casuarina trees, whose pine-shaped cones litter the sands to the delight of local children who visit each day to collect the nuts. The tranquil shallow waters of the Andaman Sea are sheltered by the curve of the bay, a 2.5-kilometre stretch of fine white sand. The feeling of space, light and beauty immediately soothes your spirit into calm relaxation and confident expectation of what this sanctuary will offer.

Uniquely different, the architecture of the hotel works in a style more akin to St Tropez or Port Grimaud than Malaysia, with all 136 rooms housed in a distinctive four-storey cream rotunda. Huge picture windows face out to the beach, pools or tropical gardens. The Lagoon Pool is an ingenious use of space, hosting a shaded salt-water and sand-bottomed pool ideal for a quiet siesta sheltering from the midday sun, and popular with adults and small children alike.

Tanjung Rhu is surrounded by 1,100 acres of waterways, mangrove swamps and beaches overlooking dramatic limestone crags. Directly in front of the beach are the islands of Pulau Pasir, Gasing and Dangli, connected at low tide to the beach by a long sand spit. It's a wonderful place to gently stroll and watch the awe-inspiring flames of the sunset, embraced by the laughter of the local people who appear from nowhere to fish.

The beach's peace is protected by the hotel's policy to allow only non-motorised vehicles – sea kayaks, catamarans and wind-surfing boards. Or a luxury yacht can be chartered for the day. Other sports activities include tennis and a wide variety of nature walks and mangrove adventures. Irshad (the naturalist from the Datai) actually trains students all over the island, some of whom work exclusively for the Tanjung Rhu. It's easy to find out which day Irshad is running a tour and ask to join the group.

Accommodation is refreshingly generous, and even the smallest Damai rooms feel spacious with a separate sitting area and balcony. Decor is simple and elegant, combining soft Thai silks with pure Indian cottons, complementing the rich brown timbers and open stone-coloured bathrooms. Nothing detracts from the external outlook. Bathrooms open out on to the bedroom with two large shutters allowing wonderfully serene views to the sea. Each has a huge oversized bath and separate power-shower room. When you wake up, the view from the Bayu rooms towards the islands has everything you'd expect from a tropical paradise. You'll see gently swaying casuarinas framed by the pale blue morning sky, a glittering turquoise sea and

(opposite) **Bayu bedroom and view.** **Reading room.**

emerald islets emerging as the sand spit slowly disappears. Langkawi at its best.

Four different restaurants, each with a spectacular beachfront location having views of the cape, present various styles of cuisine. The signature restaurant, the Rhu, specialises in fine dining and you can enjoy your meal al fresco or inside either of the air-conditioned ground or first-floor rooms. Uli, the charismatic and friendly head chef from Switzerland, has designed an east-meets-west style menu, easy on anyone's stomach. Sands is a large outdoor restaurant serving local international cuisine all day long – and here you'll find a very popular breakfast buffet. Breakfast is also served beautifully on your balcony over-

looking the sea or gardens, and is a delightfully civilised way to start the day. The Saffron is wonderful for a barefoot lunch on the terrace or less formal dinner inside, and has a great selection of simple Mediterranean specialities.

Afternoon tea in the fresh coral-white painted Reading Room is a must: hot scones and jam with a cup of Earl Grey and a chance to review at leisure the massive choice of books, CDs and videos while listening to a maestro on the grand piano as the heat of the day turns into a gentle afternoon breeze. Alternatively, sip a cocktail at any time of day at the Sunset Bar next to the breathtaking sixty-metre freshwater pool, overlooking the

beach and islands. It's also great for snack lunches by the pool.

Finally, if the romantic mood falls upon you, enjoy dinner on the beach BBQ style. A small marquee under the stars with candles, crystal and mouthwatering tastes definitely lives up to the resort's mantra, 'Heaven is under our feet as well as over our heads'.

Hidden in the grounds behind the Sunset Pool is a little hut on stilts covered in brightly coloured batiks and intricate wood carvings. Here, local artisans craft their works and encourage you to try too, offering guidance along the way. It's easy to lose an afternoon to this gentle art and a wonderful memento to take home. As you sit painting, the local

Main swimming pool. **Sands restaurant.** (opposite) **Tropical paradise.**

conversation is always philosophical and you'll be drawn into a lesson in life, gratis, by the old man with wise eyes and a wry smile.

Tanjung Rhu is one of the few resorts suitable for both the romantic escape and the full-on child (young or grown up!) escapade. There's enough space to flee from it all to claim your own stretch of paradise beach, and enough action to entertain even the most active of revellers.

Normally, only one hotel on such a tiny island would be selected for *Heaven on Earth*, representing 'the best' of what is offered – Pulau Langkawi is an exception to the rule. On the plane home, the question on every-one's lips is, 'Which is better, and where should we have stayed, the Datai or the Tanjung Rhu?' The truth is that they are quite different and offer complementary experiences.

The Datai offers an amazing rainforest experience with the benefit of a world-class spa, while the Tanjung Rhu has the most beautiful beach on the island with spacious rooms at the edge of the sea. Is it beach or rainforest? Do both and you'll really feel you got the best from Pulau Langkawi.

The Month
While temperatures and humidity are high throughout the year, January (and February too) enjoys the lowest monthly rainfall and highest number of sunshine hours, with comfortable temperatures between 22° and 33°C (73–91°F). Perfect sunbathing weather. The seas are at their calmest during this period, and golf is particularly pleasant in the afternoon breeze. If guaranteed sun and blue skies are what you're after, this is when to go.

The months of December, March and April are also very pleasant, if a little wetter.

Rains are at their worst during the monsoon season between July and October, when downpours lasting several hours each day are to be expected.

Villa Nova

Barbados

With its small patchwork quilt of fields, rugged hills and quaint yesteryear English idiosyncrasies, Barbados deserves its reputation as 'Little England'. Ladies and children still appear in their Sunday best for church and afternoon tea is served from the finest china. Impassioned cricket matches are played on the green, and squeaky-clean children dressed in immaculate starched uniforms walk to school – all are living images of the island's British legacy.

It's a legacy strengthened by the fact that Barbados never changed hands during the fierce inter-European rivalries that plagued other Caribbean territories. From the seventeenth century, when it became the first British outpost to cultivate valuable sugarcane, it remained 'the brightest jewel in the English crown'. Rural areas are still littered with the lookout towers of the old plantation houses, but sugarcane has long been supplanted with a thriving tourism industry as the number one source of income. The past few decades have seen a surge of interest in

indigenous culture – during the 1970s Rastafarianism replaced much of the historic olde-worlde Englishness, and Trafalgar Square was renamed Heroes Square in tribute to the countless lives lost in the battle for emancipation from slavery. With renewed interest in its Bajan roots, the island is keen to celebrate its traditional customs.

Throughout its history, Barbados has been protected from invasion by prevailing easterly winds and the fact that it is over 100 miles from the rest of the Lesser Antilles – an isolation giving it the name of 'the lonely island'. Not only lonely but unique, in that it is the only coral, rather than volcanic, island in the Caribbean, enjoying an individual landscape and character all of its own. On the east coast the Atlantic Ocean carries endless 'white horses' crashing to the deserted sandy beaches, a dramatic contrast to the sheltered western Caribbean side, popularly referred to as the 'platinum coast' because of its endless sandy beaches and calm waters. This highly populated coast is the main destination for

tourists and inhabitants alike. However, far from this madding crowd, high in the hills in the parish of St John, lies the Caribbean's grandest country house – a contemporary taste of historic style and splendour.

From the moment you enter Villa Nova, the atmosphere is friendly, genuine, warm and, most importantly, relaxed. Money alone could not buy the merits of such a house. Nestled in fifteen acres of lush tropical greenery, the former private plantation house named Villa Nova (literally 'new house') enjoys a rich heritage. Once the winter home of the late Earl of Avon, Sir Anthony Eden, Britain's former Prime Minister, it was also a popular haunt of Noël Coward and Sir Winston Churchill, and was visited by the Queen in 1966.

It was bought by Lynne Pemberton in 1998 and has been totally refurbished and updated by Nina Campbell, who in styling each of the twenty-seven rooms has respected the villa's former glory days. The quality of the finishes makes it virtually impossible to distinguish the

Cool veranda.   Bathroom chic.   (opposite) **Classic but contemporary bedroom.**

new from the original building. Dark stained hardwood floors, lofty ceilings with ornate mouldings and wide doors echo the character of the original house throughout. There are lovingly restored inner doors of fine lattice-work and architraves, never more conspicuous than in the ten-door drawing room which must have posed a particular challenge to furnish.

Downstairs rooms lead from one to another, where classical meets contemporary, gracefully and stylishly combining *bergère* and Chinese Chippendale chairs, modern artwork and funky cushions. In the dining room the zebra-upholstered dining chairs surround a table of local mahogany, formerly belonging to the headquarters of the British Regiment. It bears the scars of the officers' spurs where they literally put their feet up to rest.

From the veranda, you can occasionally spot green monkeys as they chatter raucously and clamber across the sweeping lawns and gardens towards the cane fields beyond. A private botanical paradise, the grounds

include mahogany trees and royal palms of neck-aching heights, banyan trees with colossal dangling roots, bearded figs and a rare cannonball tree.

All the twenty-seven bedrooms, including the three special Eden, Churchill and Haynes suites, have secluded views across the gardens. The balconies feature a combination of Lloyd Loom wicker and mahogany steamer chairs to relax in. Bathrooms are spacious, and have double vanities with white marble tops set in fine cabinets. Long claw-footed baths, large showers, fluffy white towels and Aqua Di Parma unguents abound. Some bathrooms have small porthole windows looking out on to the gardens.

At night every care is taken for your total creature comfort, with the most exemplary turn-down service to be experienced any-where. Lights are lowered, a scented candle is lit by the bedside and in the bathroom, a fresh jug of iced water is placed in the pretty Moroccan bowl next to the CD cabinet. Quiet relaxing music is set to play, a mosquito

repellent light is at work and to finish it all, the ambassador has visited to place a Ferrero Rocher on your pillow.

You may be lucky enough to meet the accomplished Lynne Pemberton, who spends many days each year at Villa Nova, or her effervescent and engaging financial adviser, Iain Jones, who spends a week a month to ensure the smooth running as well as the financial solvency of the house. You'll meet Filo the dog, a stray that had the very good taste to mooch in and make Villa Nova his home – he wanders round checking out the guests, wagging his tail at familiar faces.

(opposite) **The freshwater pool.**   **The drawing room.**

The south-facing veranda has a casual elegance and is perfect for catching the cool evening breezes during dinner. Head chef René Griffith has made an excellent name for himself creating a sophisticated menu largely based on local island produce, with specialities such as coconut and thyme soup, grilled dorado with green pea mash, and pecan pie with caramel sauce.

A new twenty-first-century spa par excellence is currently in the making, but until it is completed, spa treatments are carried out in the bedrooms. These are wonderfully transformed by Janine, the in-house therapist, with a combination of scented candles, soulful music and bowls of floating fragrant petals freshly picked from the garden. The full body treatment, incorporating hands, feet, face and scalp, uses either heated cushions or basalt volcanic rock to release any stubborn muscular tension, and the effect is both soothing and energising.

The crescent-ended black and blue tiled freshwater swimming pool, heated to body temperature, is surrounded by luxurious teak loungers in an enclosed coral-walled garden, where a profusion of brightly coloured butter-flies dance in the air. For guests wanting to travel to the coast without sacrificing Villa Nova's atmosphere and elegance, a private beach club on the west coast is in its final stages of construction for day-long relaxation by the surf.

Other facilities in the villa include an air-conditioned fitness room, a music lounge complete with Bechstein, a cocktail bar and a games-room-cum-library. Sporting activities to choose from include two resident floodlit tennis courts, golf at the famous Sandy Lane or Royal Westmoreland courses, riding, beach picnics, hiking trails with guides, day cruises on luxury catamarans, scuba diving and a selection of water sports.

Pose or repose? The choice between the showy platinum coast and this secluded leafy Eden is yours.

The Month

The optimum month to visit Villa Nova during the dry season is January, with its perfect climatic conditions. At this time of year there are fewer visitors, making it easier to get the restaurant and beach bookings of your choice, while the staff will have recovered from the hectic festive season and be able to offer a calmer, gentler service.

Being in the Caribbean, you'll need to remember when the hurricane season starts and finishes. A simple rhyme first recited to me by Graham Dear on the island explains the pattern of the hurricane season. Once learned, you'll never forget:

June too soon
July standby
August it must
September remember
October all over

This instantly eliminates five months of the calendar during the so-called wet season. But hurricanes are rare and many of the hotels are busy during the summer holidays with families happy to take the risk.

The dry season runs from December to April, during which the island's tropical climate enjoys constant hours of sunshine and temperatures at a comfortable 27°C (80°F) with cooling trade wind breezes from the north-west keeping the humidity low.

Enjoy it at its best.

February

Copacabana Palace

Rio de Janeiro

As Brazil covers more than half the landmass of South America, it's hard to decide which bit of it to experience first. This magnificent country's diverse attractions include the longest beaches in the world, the biggest river, the largest tropical rainforest and the widest waterfall, not to mention its stunning colonial towns, luxurious hotels, beautiful people – and the best carnival on earth. In summer the time difference for European travellers is a mere two hours (which means no problem with jetlag), and whether it's culture, beaches, outstanding natural beauty or adventure you're seeking, Brazil has the lot.

Rio, known by locals as the *cidade maravilhosa* or wonderful city, is instantly recognisable by its two backdrop landmarks, Corcovado and Sugarloaf Mountain. The city enjoys an interesting fusion of indigenous, white and black cultures that can be seen, and heard, cheering together in the colossal 100,000-seater Maracana Stadium, home of the city's great rivals Flamengo and Fluminense. Of course Rio is crazy about football.

Some cities have a number of world-class hotels. Rio has just one. Opened in 1923, the stucco-fronted Copacabana Palace (reminiscent of the Negresco in Nice) is considered not only by far the grandest hotel in Rio but also one of the finest in South America. It's more of a treasured national landmark than a hotel, standing in the prime location along the famous Copacabana Beach. Since its opening it's had only two owners: Octavio Guinle who built it and, since 1989, Orient-Express Hotels. If you're only happy staying in the best, this is it. As the stamping ground to the world's rich and famous, the Copa's guest book reads like a *Who's Who* directory of personalities, including Noël Coward, Albert Einstein, Walt Disney, the Rolling Stones and innumerable royalty and politicians.

Guests enter the imposing white block in the safe knowledge that they have just entered Rio's longest established hotel, the very essence of chic. Many of the 226 rooms overlook the beach or the pool – the largest in Rio – and benefit from the coveted butler service.

Recently refurbished from top to toe, the suites in the Tower Wing boast inlaid flooring, different toned cabinetry, neutral furnishings, antique prints and spacious sitting rooms with views across the South Atlantic horizon. Bathrooms are bedecked with Brazilian marble and Italian tiles with all the customary luxury amenities.

The Cipriani restaurant, open for lunch and dinner, is one of the most sophisticated in the city, offering a choice of Italian specialities designed to be as identical as possible to the dishes prepared in Venice's Cipriani Hotel. Head chef Francesco Carli is thrilled that the majority of the ingredients essential to his cooking don't have to travel so far and are found locally, so he can offer guests utterly garden-fresh produce – even the pasta is made daily.

Situated next to the pool, the Pergula restaurant is perfect for an informal al fresco buffet lunch or traditional afternoon tea. Apart from the excellent array of seafood, Rio's contribution to Brazilian cuisine is the

Junior suite and bathroom.   Semi-Olympic sized swimming pool.   (opposite) **View from Corcovado.**

feijoada, a stew consisting of bacon, salt pork and ribs, different sausages and, most essentially, the ear, tail or trotter of a pig. It's traditionally served for Saturday lunch with white rice, sliced oranges and a hot pepper sauce, but you can try it any time – and then work it off with a few laps. As well as having a semi-Olympic-sized swimming pool, the Copa is the only hotel in Rio with a rooftop tennis court as well as a gymnasium and solarium.

The true spirit of Rio reveals itself, quite literally, on the beach. Copacabana has a strong reputation for beautiful women scantily clad in G-string bikinis. Not so widely reported are Rio's arrestingly handsome men, who, like male peacocks, are dazzlingly conspicuous.

One of the first things to strike you is that the hotel seems to have more than its fair share of Adonis-like individuals – this is a hotel where the staff, and not just the guests, are notably beautiful people. Luckily, they are also well trained, knowledgeable, humorous and efficient – overseen by the Lancashire-born but Brazilian-bred general manager Philip Carruthers, admired by his team for his unassailable memory, sharp-eyed alertness and bonhomie.

Every year between 21 and 24 February, Rio closes down for *carnivali* – the benchmark against which every other carnival is compared. From the minute the keys of the city are handed over from the mayor to a

Dionysian personality named King Momo, four days of infectious boogieing, smiles and matchless festivities erupt through the streets. Neighbourhoods of all sizes take part in the revelry, and it is estimated that half a

(opposite) **Confeitaria Colombo.** **Carnival.**

million foreign visitors flock to party with the thousands of parading samba school students.

Rio has so much more to offer than the legendary carnival, though – a vibrant, pulsating, cosmopolitan city and the main cultural centre of Brazil. Very few cities in the world have combined so successfully the activities of human hurly-burly with the background of nature's beauty. The top 'must-do' excursions include a trip to Corcovado, where the 38-metre statue of Christ the Redeemer towers more than 700 metres over the whole city; a stroll through the Botanical Gardens; a cable-car ride up Sugarloaf Mountain; a walk along Copacabana Beach; a visit to the Museums of Primitive and Contemporary Art, reached by boat; and an atmospheric lunch in the downtown shopping district at the Confeitaria

Colombo where the Art Nouveau charm provides a living portrait of Rio's *belle époque*.

With today's very favourable exchange rate, you can shop till you drop for leather clothing, shoes and handbags and hardly feel the hole in your pocket – it's only sensible to take an extra suitcase.

All in all, Rio is a city you have to see. A perfect combination for a culture and beach break would be a trip to lively Rio followed by a restful stay in the historic village of Paraty, affording the most authentic taste of the real Brazil. With a little extra time, you could extend your trip to include the Pantanal, South America's main wildlife sanctuary. Larger than France, it's home to the greatest area of flora and fauna on earth, where you can even go piranha fishing or alligator spotting.

The Month
Brazil's annual average temperature is approximately 28°C (low 80sF) in the north and 20°C (65–70°F) in the south, with the rainy season stretching between November and March in the Rio area. February is the perfect month for both climate and festivities – and *carnivali* occurs each year during the four days before Ash Wednesday.

The carnival month of February has a vibrant, colourful excitement all of its own. Streets are full of exuberant energy as spontaneous parades absorb every pair of limbs to join the fun. The Samba parade in the huge Sambadrome draws thousands of participants in extravagant costumes to create the party of a lifetime and gives a whole new slant to the song 'Lola, she was a show girl...'

Pousada Marquesa

Brazil

Venturing 250 kilometres south of Rio, you'll hit the breakpoint between the city's urban sprawl and the green coast's enchanting rural bliss. It lies somewhere south of Mangaratiba, where the rambling suburbs shrink to sub-suburbs which in turn transform into small seaside resorts hugging the land between the opaque blanket of tropical forest and horseshoe-shaped sandy bays.

Set on the edge of the Costa Verde National Park – Brazil's ancient Atlantic rainforest and one of the country's most beautiful areas – the Indian trail known as the Caminho do Ouro, or Gold Route, leads into the small town of Paraty.

Built in the sixteenth century as a transhipment point for the gold cargo en route to Portugal, Paraty was once the second most important port in Brazil. When the gold trade ceased, the port was abandoned and a new inland route through Minais Gerais was established. By the time Paraty was rediscovered in the 1960s, the surrounding area was a fiercely protected national park and the town was declared a Unesco world heritage site.

Left forgotten, 350-year-old Paraty has remained untouched by modernisation. Today this small coastal town is a virtual museum hidden in tropical glory. Within its historic walls, the cobbled streets, banked with grand old colonial houses, have hardly changed. Some of the houses have been transformed into candlelit gourmet restaurants, trendy bars, haute couture outlets and artists' studios. Seventeen of them have been fashioned into chic townhouse *pousadas*, which is Brazilian for bed and breakfast. With a little under 600 inhabitants, the entire population could just about fill all the rooms of the inns.

There are subtle signs of movement on every corner but on Sundays the whole town bursts into life. Congregations from the ubiquitous churches overflow into the squares from all directions and the great green doors of Nossa Senhora dos Remédios remain open throughout the mass as children, dogs and the odd chicken come and go, to the amusement of old men sitting on benches.

Located in Mother Church Square, the Pousada Marquesa is one of the oldest and prettiest inns in Paraty. Every room is furnished with the original antique furniture redolent of the port's colonial history and importance. The Marquesa has a rustic air of a bygone age and best typifies the untouched charm of the town.

Behind the plain whitewashed façade the music and sitting rooms both contain a charmingly quirky collection of seventeenth and eighteenth-century antiques, oil lamps, statues and paintings. The breakfast room, with its wide mahogany floorboards and a line of brightly coloured sash windows, is chock-a-block with different sized wall clocks all chiming at different times.

Within the courtyard garden, next to the small, shaded swimming pool, the cosy Captain's Bar festooned with a variety of curious seafaring objects is a lovely spot to retreat to after an active day at sea.

Bedrooms are simple but everything is authentic: large antique beds, oak coffers,

(opposite) **Fishing boats along the pier.** **Quiet cobbled streets.** **Antique furniture from a bygone era.**

cane rocking chairs, and pieces of extraordinary historical value in eighteenth-century Brazilian colonial style. I recommend you take the hotel's only suite or one of the two rooms overlooking the square and the church. The latter movingly pipes out the hallowed musical tones of the *Ave Maria* at dusk.

Each morning, the Marquesa serves a continental-style breakfast – the fresh papaya with lime is perfection as are the freshly baked cakes, but that's about it. Fortunately Paraty has plenty of restaurants to choose from and two of the best are close by. The upmarket and very chic Restaurante Porto specialises in sophisticated fusion food and has been recognised in dining compendiums across the globe. Right opposite the Marquesa, the Italian restaurant Punto Di Vino has a beautiful enclosed garden and serves excellent pizza cooked in a traditional wood oven.

Try the local cuisine. Traditional dishes like *peixe azu* (blue fish) are as tempting to the eye as they are to the palate. Locals also boast about the famous *pinga* (*cachaça*), which was synonymous with Paraty and the name of the town for many years.

The people of Paraty are some of the friendliest and most generous anywhere in the world. It's common for locals to want to give you something as a present – either a *caipirinha* (Brazil's national drink) on the house; an extra little hand-carved boat once you've chosen the one you want; or free entry to a museum. It's as if they just can't help but give and is very refreshing if somewhat bewildering to cynical westerners.

The Marquesa also has its own schooner, the *Sir Francis Drake*, a specially rigged fishing boat perfect for a scenic voyage through the sixty-five islands scattered along the length of the bay fringing Paraty. Many have fantastic desert island beaches, and the warm waters hold the largest number of species of dolphin in the world and a wealth of tropical fish. Sipping a *caipirinha* as you gently sail back to the port while watching the sun set on the islands is as close to paradise as you'll find.

After a long, hard day on the schooner, it's definitely worth stopping off at the Kontiki restaurant situated on the Duas Irmãs Island, just ten minutes from Paraty's port. It serves authentic Spanish paella, as well as other Mediterranean delicacies.

It's fair to say the *pousada* is not a five-star residence – in fact it's barely three – but the level of comfort is fine. Given the choice between an all-singing all-dancing beach resort or the unique sanctuary of a town virtually unaffected by the twenty-first century, there's no contest. May this little gem remain an unspoilt idyll forever.

The Month

Like Rio, Paraty's average temperature is approximately 20°C (65–70F°). February is the perfect month to enjoy the climate and festivities of *carnivali*. The town celebrates its anniversary on the 28th, with a huge party, plenty of *caipirinhas* and dancing in the street.

Ladera

St Lucia

Columbus was the first European to spot St Lucia – though, in his haste to reach South America, he didn't stop. It was the French who were the first Europeans to claim it as their own, quickly contested by the British. The island changed hands over a dozen times between the two before finally resting in British hands in 1814 – and gaining independence in 1979 while remaining in the Commonwealth.

Despite its history, St Lucia feels more French than English in character; the strong Franco-Creole cultural influences are recognised in the cuisine, the musical patois spoken by the locals and the prevailing Catholic faith. Villages and towns have predominantly French names, and the inspiration for the island's fêted poems and dances is etched on the faces and hearts of its inhabitants.

Nowadays tourism has replaced agriculture as the main source of income for local people. The island's two giant volcanic peaks – the Pitons, cloaked in lush tropical rain-forest – rise straight out of the sea to a towering

800 metres, standing proud as if to signify St Lucia's supreme popularity as a Caribbean destination. The island's roads are full of stomach-gripping hairpin bends where men pull giant boa constrictors from sacks and wave them round their heads hoping for a dollar for their bravery. As the twisting journey passes the port of Soufrière the sweet smell of coconut oil from the factory softens the senses, while the sign outside the cemetery – which ponders, 'I'm here, who's next?' – soon awakens them. Life is an adventure here.

Sheltered by the sapphire crystalline waters, many of the undisturbed sandy coves, which vary from blinding white to shining ebony, can be reached only by yacht. While much of the dense emerald green rainforest that blankets St Lucia is still untouched, the island's fertile soil is home to acres of banana crops and figs, while frangipani, mangoes, hibiscus, bamboo and orchids line the roadway.

It is in a location such as this, on the south-western tip of St Lucia, that the treetop retreat

of Ladera has evolved. Two miles from Soufrière, perched high on a hilltop ridge bang between the Pitons overlooking the glittering waters of Anse des Pitons, is the Caribbean's finest mountain retreat. The American designer John Di Pol not only had a good eye for location but was ahead of his time in his sympathetic incorporation of local materials, using a sensitive combination of Caribbean timbers, local stone and terracotta tiles.

As you enter your bedroom, prepare your-self for a view of a lifetime. Uniquely, each of the six villas and nineteen suites has been designed without a fourth wall, thus encompassing the island's most breathtaking view as part of the decor. This inimitable way of capturing the area's magnificent natural beauty into every room, while maintaining complete privacy and shelter from the elements, bestows the escapist atmosphere of a giant tree house. The total absence of windowpanes or sliding doors allows the full

Suite with a view. (opposite) **The Heliconia flower.**

power of the Pitons' presence into the room and terrace, with the added luxury of being able to slip effortlessly into your private plunge or swimming pool without interrupting your mesmerised gaze. Just before dusk humming-birds gather around the hedge at the foot of the gardens darting in and out of the pintas blossoms.

Bedrooms rich in polished woods are furnished with hand-carved four-poster beds draped with flowing bug nets (it's too high for mosquitoes), large pieces of teak and French antique furniture, wicker chairs, and St Lucian artwork. Local artisans have individually crafted each of the bathrooms. Taps have been replaced with brightly decorated hand-carved wooden fish and a conch shell substitutes as a spout. Even the

large showers are open, overlooking the amphitheatre of tropical vegetation.

Moving outside, leading from reception, there's a botanical garden walk directed by numbered posts corresponding to a list of plant species. It passes huge bushes of pinwheel jasmine, vanilla orchids, snow in the mountain and heliconias – Ray, the gardener, is delighted to escort any enthusiasts along the way.

All the staff at Ladera wear cheery smiles and the same vibrant coloured gingham that furnishes the tables and chairs. Below the Tcholit (tree frog) Bar is the open-walled Dasheene restaurant, named after the thousands of dasheene plants (a cross between an Irish spud and a sweet potato) that were once cultivated on the site. Orlando Satchel,

a renowned Caribbean chef, has created an innovative self-styled Nouvelle Caribbean cuisine composed largely of fresh native ingredients, most of which have been grown or caught in the immediate neighbourhood. Among the mouthwatering flavours synonymous with St Lucia are Derek Walcott accra cakes and green figs, a tasty banana fishcake with Creole sauce and sweet potato fries, and warm pumpkin and coconut pudding. Looking out from a balcony table as the view changes with every shift of light, the stunning backdrop of the Pitons presents a visual paradise which enduces a state of total relaxation.

Dr Dolittle had plenty of time to relax and talk to the animals during his filming in Marigot Bay further up the coast, but the scene from your bedroom 'window' is so

(opposite) **Villa Pool and Pitons.**   **Yachts in Marigot Bay.**

restful, it's hard to summon the energy to escape the serenity of the rainforest and refreshing cool breezes to explore the surrounding area.

However, if you do manage to tear yourself away, a few minutes' drive from Ladera will take you to the characteristic gingerbread architecture of the sun-faded houses in the sleepy fishing port of Soufrière – the region's capital – where brightly coloured fishing boats bob in the water along the beach front. Closer still to Ladera are the sulphurous boiling mud pools in the world's only 'drive-in' volcano, where many people bathe hoping for the healing powers of the steaming waters. The vapours can occasionally be smelt in the early morning and late evening from your bedroom terrace, reminding you of Ladera's volcanic location.

A regular complimentary shuttle between Ladera and the pretty Anse des Pitons is offered throughout the day. Snorkelling along the beach or scuba diving on the colourful coral walls of the Pitons among the turtles, seahorses and angel fish, you'll encounter a dazzling cross-section of marine life – not to be missed.

If you're feeling adventurous, take a day to climb Gros Piton with a qualified guide – the views from the top are unforgettable. Down at sea level, it is easy to charter a yacht for the day to watch the spinner and bottlenose dolphins, humpback, pilot and sperm whales that are regularly spotted throughout the year. But really there's nothing better to do than sit back on your sun lounger, relax, and soak up the captivating view from your private terrace.

The Month

St Lucia benefits from a tropical climate with relatively constant hours of sunshine, and temperatures ranging from 18° to 30°C (mid-60s to mid-80s F), although during the hottest time of the year between June and August temperatures reach 35°C (mid-90s F). The rainy season, between June and October, experiences most of the average rainfall, which pounds the mountain tops, mainly in short heavy bursts. February is traditionally the driest month with sweet cool breezes from the trade winds, and the hummingbirds are plentiful in the hibiscus bushes – days are pleasantly hot and evenings are cool. The exuberant Christmas and New Year crowds have long departed and life has returned to its natural pace.

March

Four Seasons

New York

As long as I can remember, New York has been known as the Big Apple, the city that never sleeps, with its familiar silhouette of the world's most distinguished skyscrapers. It's slick, loud, sometimes brash and always fun, pulsating with life and run with multi-national blood. For the last three centuries thousands have dreamt of turning their rags to riches and, as the song says, if you can make it there you'll make it anywhere.

Manhattan Island is a grid of long avenues flanked with skyscrapers, characterised by hectic roads erupting with steam from air vents and pinstriped roller-bladers with brief-cases avoiding traffic jams. In the heart of this concrete jungle Central Park lies low like a giant green empty Lego board-base with its perpendicular sides and horizontal stage. This oversized quadrangle of foliage serves as New York's release valve, absorbing cyclists, horses and carriages, hot air balloons, walkers, roller-bladers and joggers, with perfect poise.

If you're looking to be impressed, the hotel that best epitomises New York City is the Four

Seasons, the thrusting skyscraper designed by acclaimed architect I. M. Pei. Its tapering fifty-two storeys occupy the entire depth between 57th and 58th Streets, rising high above Manhattan's premier shopping district between Park and Madison Avenues. Graduated slender setbacks lit by forty-six lanterns stretch neck-achingly into a towering skyscraper, earning it a place on the celebrated skyline. Classic French Mangy limestone, also used by the same architect on Paris's Louvre expansion, adds to the impression of volume and height and post-modernist contemporary élan.

Entering the building inspires all the emotions a skyscraper should – thrill, exhilaration, excitement and wonder as the imposing 7-metre glass and stone doorway opens on to an equally awesome marble foyer with a gaping backlit onyx ceiling. Described by Pei as an urban theatre, the raised lounge areas dominated by huge urns filled with springtime forsythia make an affable state-ment, lifting the otherwise slick city aura around the beech-panelled reception desk.

Staff instantly glide to welcome you, mark-ing specific personal preferences in code on your registration details. They want to know if you smoke, are a city fresher, like wake-up calls or want a valet service to help you unpack.

Rooms are spread over the fifty-five floors, accessed by two banks of lifts. Vertigo sufferers may find the dizzy heights of the upper floors too much, but the panoramic views over Central Park and the city skyline are worth getting a little light-headed for. Do try to take a room or suite in the tower overlooking the park – the picture windows provide a panoramic view on a rare scale.

Modernist Deco rooms are a minimum 55 square metres, with walk-in closets that guzzle your suitcases, and plush peach marble bathrooms with Niagara-pressured plumbing and Bulgari bubbles. There's no time to dawdle filling the bath – a rapido sixty seconds and you'll be flooding the ballroom. Throughout the suites customised furniture and cabinetry of English sycamore, beech and maple contribute to the warm, uncluttered, contemporary decor,

(opposite) **The awesome marble foyer.** **Modernist Deco suite.**

with distinctive signed prints by Le Corbusier and Mariani lining the beige walls.

It's truly uplifting to visit a hotel that fully understands the value of a good night's sleep. Sealy beds are fitted with lightweight duvets, and guests have a choice of pillows including buckwheat-filled neck pillows. Windows open even on the fifty-second floor, and electronic curtains are sensitively fitted with blackout interiors.

Service is where Four Seasons really make their mark, and their legendary standards are today's benchmark for hotels around the globe.

If you are one of those people who have problems remembering names thirty seconds after you've been introduced, you'll be startled by the concierge who manages to remember the name of every guest staying in the 368 rooms. I sometimes wonder if your name is furtively lasered on to your forehead at check-

in and read with a secret Matrix-style device by staff – but it's not just names they're good at.

During my last stay I asked Kenny, in concierge, to make a lunch reservation downtown; the restaurant was full but, unfazed, he took my mobile number saying he knew the maitre d', and sure enough he called thirty minutes later to confirm a table by the window. The same thing happened at dinner.

Fine service even extends to housekeeping where you'll find thumbed corners of your novel are straightened and courteously replaced with considerate bookmarks.

When it comes to eating in hotels, New Yorkers are by and large ambivalent. Fifty Seven Fifty Seven at the Four Seasons proves to be an exception to the rule, presenting inventive contemporary American cuisine with regional and Mediterranean twangs. Executive chef Brooke Vosika, a twenty-year

veteran of Four Seasons Hotels and Resorts, describes his dishes as 'layers of flavours brought out from singular ingredients'. For bored tastebuds try the vegetable bell pepper steak with chanterelles and arugula, and for something completely different the strawberry and tapioca soup with lemon tequila sorbet.

An amusing list of pre-dinner drinks, including the famous Four Seasons' Big Apple Martinis and eleven types of champagne cocktail coloured blue, pink, green and red to suit your mood, is served in the trendy open bar which is separated from the restaurant by a stunning beech-framed circular window. Decor is theatrical, with polished maple floors and walls covered in mustard-toned fabric, interspersed with six elevated windows overlooking 58th Street, while the comfortable Dakota Jackson chairs and

The champagne bar.   Main dining room.   (opposite) The Piano Bar.

cherry tabletops echo the pattern used on the floor.

Other meal options include the lobby lounge, which is ideal for a quick lunch or pre-theatre, serving an ingenious three-piece sip, dip and roll menu combining *bouche*-size portions of soup, brochettes and wraps.

The compact 450-square-metre spa and fitness centre includes a steam room, sauna, whirlpool and massage suite offering a menu of treatments including massage, facials, waxing, manicures and pedicures. Unsurprisingly popular, the jet-lag remedy focuses on a quick recovery after time in the air and incorporates an aromatherapy massage, hydrating facial and paraffin foot treatment – book before you leave home, as the locals love it as much as overseas visitors do.

Many of New York's most famous sights are within a few minutes' walk of the hotel. You

can take your pick from thousands of shops and over 150 museums and galleries including Carnegie Hall, the Rockefeller Center, MOMA, Tiffany's, FAO Schwarz, The Frick, Guggenheim and the Metropolitan Museums.

Shopping is synonymous with New York, and nearby Bergdorf Goodman values the patronage of Four Seasons guests a good deal – so much so that they arrange exclusive after-hours shopping cocooned from the hullabaloo.

Broadway is packed with shows and musicals all year round. Among the classics is a pure New York extravaganza guaranteed to get your toes tapping – *Movin' Out*, a musical based around Billy Joel's musical hits.

Whatever you decide to do during the day, kick off your vagabond shoes and be king of the hill, top of the heap, and spend a night in the city's tallest hotel with a character that literally screams New York.

The Month
New York's climate is changeable, with moderate rainfall throughout the year. Winter endures a big freeze and snow is almost guaranteed; heat waves are common during the summer months with soaring temperatures for days on end. Springtime enters New York in a flurry of colour offering bright clear skies, crisp fresh morning breezes and open-air markets selling seasonal blossoms. The park becomes alive again with fresh growth sprouting all around – skaters enjoy the last of the ice on the open-air rink and it's just warm enough to enjoy an al fresco brunch.

March hosts a variety of events including the Art Expo, New York Flower Show and the Saint Patrick's Day Irish-American parade. Overall it's the perfect month to explore the city on foot and browse museums and shops before the busy tourist season begins.

Chalet Eugenia

Switzerland

Klosters is uncontested by those in the know as Europe's most sophisticated ski resort – home to one of the most diverse ski areas yet retaining all the charm of a traditional Swiss alpine village. Everything about this small resort is refreshingly understated, and is probably the reason for the long-established royal patronage.

Fantastic skiing opportunities offer slopes for all ages and abilities, ranging from the stunning tree-lined Kublis to the family-orientated nucleus around Madrisa. Dining on the slopes is always a romantic joy, especially when you're taken to one of the secluded mountain restaurants by timeless horse-drawn sleigh. Klosters offers the ski experience of yesteryear with undreamt-of peace and comfort – and Chalet Eugenia epitomises it all, from the very first moment you're welcomed by smiling staff into its cosy, relaxed atmosphere.

Built by Baroness Thyssen-Bornemisza in the resort's early years, this seasoned mountain chalet remains the family's winter residence for a couple of weeks each year; the rest of the time it's available to anyone wanting to indulge in alpine perfection. Situated in a prime position adjacent to the nursery slopes, it is only a five-minute walk or a two-minute chauffeured drive to the shops, bars and restaurants in the village.

Each of the six individually designed ensuite bedrooms is utter hedonism embedded with local charm and the warmth of wood everywhere. Original period features accentuate the alpine escapism, and swathes of beams and exposed floors covered in Aubusson rugs, furs and polished antique oak coffers all contribute to the cosy comfort.

Most of the bedrooms have south-facing balconies, and four have open fires that gently glow and crackle as you drift to sleep. Luxury abounds with fresh flowers, thick fluffy bathrobes, scented candles, slippers, duck-down pillows and Penhaligon bubbles.

Several acres of snowy pasture separate Eugenia from its nearest neighbour down the slope, so the long-reaching southerly views over the impressive Gotschna are unadulterated chocolate box perfection. Some moments are so paralysingly dazzling that it's hard to pull yourself away from the window.

After a hard day's skiing everyone congregates on the first floor in the huge drawing room around the pillared central fireplace, devouring fresh cakes and copious cups of gluwein. There's also a snug television room and elegant panelled library to escape to.

Skiing all day certainly cultivates a healthy appetite, and Eugenia's connoisseur chefs ensure that the activities on the slopes are well rewarded with a hearty feast each night. Before dinner, chilled Veuve Cliquot flows freely to crown or commiserate with your performance on the slopes. Dinner is served in the stunning timbered dining room or occasionally in the adjacent smaller dining room equipped with the original wood-fired oven. After the third or fourth night most guests opt out of the six-course dinner and beg the chef to prepare something a little friendlier to the waistband –

(opposite) **Drawing room with pillared central fireplace.**   **Hallway.**

you really can have too much of a good thing. A typical menu is full of flavours to savour, like sea food lasagne, followed by lemon and champagne sorbet, pan-fried ostrich with polenta, a trio of raspberry treats and a selection of French and Swiss cheeses, accompanied by a delectable selection of fine international wines carefully chosen to complement each meal. And if you're still hungry, there's coffee by the fire with irresistible petits fours.

If you can tear yourself away from the log fires and enveloping sofas to eat out one evening, the two-star Michelin Walserhof – Prince Charles's favourite – or the lively Chésa Grishuna are charming alternatives.

Sumptuous surroundings are so often let down by shoddy service. Not here. Great care has been taken to recruit professional staff from the finest restaurants and hotels across Europe. An attentive team, including a chauffeur, two chefs, a general manager and an

assistant, all dedicate themselves to assuring you have everything you could possibly need – not a grumpy codger or bleary-eyed gap-year student to be seen.

What really makes a difference is having your own chauffeur. It's never been so easy to get on the slopes. The general manager informs you at breakfast each morning where the best skiing for the day is according to weather conditions and forecasts. At the end of the day you simply call your chauffeur to

Master bathroom with crackling fire.   (opposite) **The timbered dining room.**

pick you up. He'll discreetly find your skis while you're sipping your hot chocolate, pack them in the 4x4 and you won't see them again until the next day.

Between Klosters and Davos there are over 300 kilometres of pistes, while Madrisa's newly opened Kids Land aims to satisfy the heart's desire of the under tens. Cross-country skiers can glide across tracks that are groomed daily, and walkers can hike through local hamlets stopping to taste local specialities.

For tired aching bones, every Swiss doctor recommends twenty minutes in the sauna or steam room – Eugenia has both – but for something a little extra guests have

complimentary access to the fabulous spa at the Hotel Vereina which is located just down the hill from Eugenia. The hotel's new wellness and beauty clinic has a large swimming pool kept at a delicious 29°C, fully equipped fitness room, traditional Finnish sauna with a crushed ice fountain, four aromatherapy steam rooms and a variety of Thalasso therapies.

Chalet Eugenia is a jewel in the crown of Descent International. When Englishman Kit Harrison created this unique ski concept, his dream was to create a chalet experience that would immerse his guests in unrivalled luxury far beyond the reach of five-star hotels.

Little did he know how successful his vision would prove. Be warned: once you've skied Descent style there's no going back!

The Month
As global climatic conditions have changed, so has the snow. It is generally accepted that March is yesteryear's February in the Alps. There have been record late falls of snow in recent years, and while no one can accurately predict what is going to happen from year to year, locals acknowledge that the optimum month for the finest skiing conditions – snow combined with crisp warm sunshine – is undoubtedly March.

Rawlins Plantation Inn

St Kitts

Belonging to the Leeward Islands of the West Indies archipelago, St Kitts is a relatively young volcanic island, separated from Nevis by a slender channel only three kilometres wide – appropriately known as the 'Narrows', notorious for its perilous seas as well as renowned for its magnificent coral reefs. St Kitts has stunning views of neighbouring islands, but is itself one of the sleepiest in the Caribbean; the beaches are deserted, and streets and villages are free of the ritzy-glitzy glamour seen elsewhere in the region. Yet St Kitts exudes a strange sense of belonging, and first-time visitors often feel they're coming home.

From the tarmac of the spanking new airport you'll pass through the quaint capital, bustling beautiful Basseterre, which has preserved its architecture of ornate ginger-bread carpentry and sympathetically restored many of its eighteenth-century buildings. Renowned for its cleanliness, safety and tidiness, it is full of monuments, parks and public areas. Today it is a hub of activity where

locals and visitors assemble in the crossroads around the Circus or in Independence Square – a pretty, open area with pathways designed in the pattern of the Union Jack.

South of Basseterre around Frigate Bay, new resort hotels are starting to spring up, but fortunately they are localised to this small indent, leaving the rest of the island untouched and in peace. And nowhere is more peaceful than what must be the Caribbean's most nostalgic hideaway hotel: Rawlins.

Sitting in twenty acres of lawned gardens and 350 feet above sea level on the slopes of Mount Liamuiga, Rawlins is surrounded by fields of swaying sugar cane. Its main dwelling is a converted seventeenth-century sugar plantation house, one of only two remaining on the island and home to the hotel owners. In the grounds, various outbuildings have been transformed into just ten detached, cottage-style suites, including a split-level lava rock wind-mill, which has a dreamy upstairs bedroom and downstairs sitting room and bathroom.

Speckled all over the manicured lawns below are the ubiquitous white egrets standing like props from an *Alice in Wonderland* croquet game. You feel your shoulders relax as you're given your un-losable brick-sized door key to enter a world of utter serenity.

Each cottage is decorated in a locally appealing and simple style with exposed wooden floorboards, stone or whitewashed walls, fresh, brightly coloured Caribbean cotton upholstery and linen sheets on planter-style four-poster beds, interspersed with rugs and family antiques. Pillows smell as freshly wind-dried linen should. The bathrooms reflect the old-fashioned virtues of the property, brimming with uncommon niceties such as linen-covered dressing tables adorned with hand-picked posies. Claire Rawlins, co-owner of the hotel with her husband Paul, is herself Kittian – her ancestry dates back to seventeenth-century tales of a Huguenot missionary named Mallalieu – and you'll readily detect her

The terrace dining room. **Croquet on the lawn.** (opposite) **Lava rock windmill.**

family's evocative influences throughout the cottages and plantation house.

Air-conditioning, telephones, mini-bars and satellite television are nowhere to be seen – the focus is on more innocent pleasures: verandas under gingerbread eaves with swinging hammocks in which to enjoy the ever present breezes; restful enclaves for delving into one of the myriad books from the main house; and acres of landscaped gardens rich in lush tropical species of plant and fauna to explore.

Paul and Claire guard the relaxation and privacy of their guests in perfect measure. There is plenty of lively conversation and conviviality between guests on the wide veranda at mealtimes, but other than that they are left to wallow in unadulterated escapism. If you're not in love, or happy in your own company, don't even think of coming – this is no Vegas.

Claire's ambrosial food is flavourful Kittian with an Escoffier flair, matched by Paul's passion for fine wine. Her cooking is among the healthiest, most interesting and delicate in the West Indies, often using her own kitchen garden ingredients. A tantalising buffet-style lunch is spread out each day in the terrace dining room – built on the ruins of the old boiling house – comprising a palette of colourful dishes whose secret recipes have been passed down through the generations: saltfish, candied sweet potatoes with walnuts, and conch ravioli to name but a few.

Afternoon tea or pre-dinner aperitifs are best enjoyed sitting in one of the comfy armchairs on the wide veranda of the house overlooking the north-western horizon as the sun goes down behind the island of St Eustatius, turning the sky into a tequila sunrise of pomegranate crimson, orange and gold.

The planter's-style dinner served on Claire's Royal Doulton is a set four-course affair, taking account of each guest's personal preference. One delicacy Paul longs for is wine gums, impossible to source anywhere in the Caribbean (make his day and take some out with you – I'm sure you'll receive a very good cocktail in return!).

Within the grounds are a croquet lawn (watch out for those egrets), a small spring-fed

(opposite) **Drawing room.** **Lemon Grass bedroom.**

swimming pool, a grass tennis court and dozens of footpaths leading up through the sugar cane towards the rainforest.

The island's most celebrated artist, Kate Spencer, has her studio – a large converted barn – adjacent to the grounds of Rawlins. It was in fact her husband Philip who lovingly restored the house (his ancestral home) before selling it to Paul and Claire, and he's now restoring the huge yacht you see in the lower barn.

An interesting way to spend a morning is aboard the distinctive sugar train, which boards at Needsmust Station and circumnavigates the sparsely populated island in just over three hours. Originally designed in 1912 to deliver sugar cane from the fields to the mill at Basseterre, the converted railcars hug the coastline and roll across deep ghuts winding through abandoned villages and once lucrative plantations.

The island endured a long and volatile period of French and British occupation before finally resting in British hands. Standing testament to its history on the upper north-western side of the island lies the Brimstone Hill Fortress, a UNESCO world heritage site, which took 106 years of slave labour to build and is considered the Gibraltar Rock of the West Indies – it gives impressive views from the top. Nevis, easily seen from the south of the island, can be quickly reached by plane or boat and makes a perfect day trip.

If it all sounds just too energetic, you could simply let yourself unwind and allow the days to pass quietly by as you *lime* away in your hammock cooled by the gentle breezes.

The Month
Unlike many other islands, sunshine is virtually guaranteed every day of the year in St Kitts, averaging 8.3 hours per day – amazing even by Caribbean standards. The heady delight of this climatic norm is in sobering contrast to the misery of the abnormal number of hurricanes the island has experienced in the last decade. The island is prone to a wide range of micro-climates influenced by the north-easterly winds, according to the location, altitude and orientation, but humidity is low all year round.

While February can be rather windy, locals love March for its settled weather and clear blue skies; the fields are bustling with the sugar harvest, and elsewhere the poinsettias are still in flower and hibiscus and frangipani blooms cover the roadways.

For a complete contrast, St Kitts is probably best combined with another Caribbean island such as St Barthélemy or Barbados, mixing complete sanctuary with something a little more vivacious.

April

Blakes Hotel

Amsterdam

For many people, Amsterdam means tulips, postcard images of windmills, diamonds, Edam cheese, clogs, canals and bridges – along with its renowned tolerance and freedom. Fewer people are aware that it is also home to Rembrandt's *Night Watch* and Van Gogh's *Sunflowers*, and has more museums per square mile than any other city in the world.

As metropolises go, Amsterdam offers all the enchantment of a compact city where everything is within walking distance, without forgoing any major city attractions. It is crammed with history, culture, entertainment and cuisine from all corners of the earth. Different quarters host flea markets, antique and art markets and, of course, beautiful flower markets crammed with tulips of every colour. Rather than walk, most people choose to get around by pedal power (600,000 bicycles at the last count), and the streets ring with the tring-a-ling of handlebar bells. People cycle to work, to the shops or to school, and even policemen and delivery men go around on two wheels.

During the eighteenth century the city evolved around a circular grid of canals, resulting in a stylish collage of imperial architecture. Each new resident made his mark by designing a distinctive blueprint for each façade and gable, producing Amsterdam's characterful cityscape.

Located in the heart of the finest archi-tectural quarter on the Keizersgracht, or Emperor's Canal (one of the grandest and most famous canals), Blakes is slightly secluded from the street by a private cobbled courtyard ornamented with immaculate box topiary. The four original seventeenth-century town-houses have had a chequered history – once a famous theatre, then almshouses, then a mansion house – and have now undergone another metamorphosis. Through the sand-stone portico, the early-seventeenth-century Van Campen's doorway leads to a definitively twenty-first-century minimalist black and white lobby area. Surprisingly, the two styles blend together effortlessly – but this is Amsterdam, 'the young person's city of

Europe'. The sleek contemporary decor perfectly complements the architectural beauty made possible by the lucrative trading with the Dutch East Indies during Holland's Golden Age.

British designer Anouska Hempel has cleverly linked the hotel's interior with the city's rich colonial culture – decorating it in her stylish contemporary minimalism, predominantly in black and white with dark beamed ceilings, brick floors and black-rimmed sisal rugs. East meets west, young meets old, ying meets yang, black meets white – a Zen-den of exclusive comfort.

Blakes' seventy-two catwalk-handsome staff – young, sleek and dressed in black – are a truly international team drawn from twenty-six nationalities. There isn't a language they can't speak between them. Initial impressions are often fixed by the first face you see and Bart, 'as in Simpson', is instantly friendly and welcoming, taking great care to ensure his visitors' comfort and satisfaction. The team is headed by Spanish-born Richard van

Canal facing suite.

Batenburg, who has been at the hotel since its inception and is well versed in accommodating the needs of a discerning international clientele.

Most of the forty-one bedrooms surround the peaceful inner courtyard garden and many have a view overlooking the quiet canal street. They have been decorated in colour schemes reflecting various oriental ingredients – a blue and white room paying tribute to Chinese porcelain; white and beige for ginger spice; green for jade; and polished chic burgher black and white corridors. Four-poster beds are draped in linen and silks and swathed in blankets and cushions.

As you enter the bedroom, gentle tones of classical music emanate from a lacquered cabinet, where a mini bar stacked with the normal grapes and grains also includes some unusual additions. You'll find remedies such as a 'snog me senseless' breath spray,

a 'bender mender' hangover cure and an OPUR pure oxygen cylinder – partying is obviously on the menu.

At night, smoky glass bottles with enamel stoppers are filled with Blakes' own brand of fizzy and still water and placed by each bed, and the down-lighters are dimmed to a softer hue. Hempel's signature accessories include towering bedside lamps – 1.5 metres tall – placed on Balinese tables, and a butler's-tray writing table decorated with a single white orchid on a grey slate mat.

Each bedroom is separated by slatted mahogany screens from the bathroom, where basins have been replaced by sloping lime-stone channels fitted with tiny chrome taps and a wand-shaped hand-shower attachment. Every detail, no matter how minor, follows the integrity of the design mapped out by Hempel's vision of modernity marrying antiquity. Black and cream lacquered trunks discreetly hide

piles of blankets, and symmetrically lined rattan and bamboo furniture add an echo of empire with an Indonesian dimension.

While the adventurous and financially fruitful Golden Age has long since passed, Indonesia's influence is still seen in the

streets of Amsterdam with a wealth of popular and fashionable restaurants devoted to its cuisine. It's particularly worth sampling in Blakes' own highly regarded restaurant. Sited in an old bakery, it is simply furnished with black tables and chairs, original herringbone brick floors and walls studded with the old bakers' ovens. Tables are dressed with pots of fragrant thyme bushes and crested Chateau de Bagnols chinaware.

Executive Chef Schilo van Coevorden has created a sensational fusion menu also encompassing the diet-breaking temptations of Italian and Thai cuisine. The menu includes delights such as a black lacquered seafood box of wok-tossed soft-shell crab with pomelo salad and lobster dim sum, followed by foie gras soup with mouthwatering goose-liver tortellini. House specials include a king-size soufflé served to unsuspecting guests to the huge amusement of onlookers – finish it if you can!

Once away from the dining table, there's so much to do in the city that you're spoilt for choice. If you're not feeling energetic, then an hour-long canal cruise is an absolute must, passing under some of the 1,281 bridges in the city. Otherwise, the most enjoyable way to get around is to take out one of the hotel's black licence-plated bicycles to explore the streets – which makes for quick and easy access to the city's intimate 'brown bars' and the wonders of the Van Gogh and Rijksmuseum. A visit to the Anne Frank Museum is a memorable and moving experience. Based at the house in which she wrote her famous diary while hiding from the Nazis during the Second World War, it incorporates interactive technology that takes you on an emotionally stirring virtual journey.

Whatever you do in the city, there is plenty of theatre left at 384 Keizersgracht, and to stay here is to play a role in its day-to-day evolution.

The Month
The clogs might have all but disappeared but the famous blooms have not. April is a month filled with tulips and is the best time to marvel at the twenty-eight hectares of bulbs at the Keukenhof Gardens. On 30 April each year there's a huge street party and carnival to celebrate Queen's Day and the city is decked in orange as parades pass through, culminating in a spectacular firework display. Amsterdam recognises the importance of its museums and offers free entry to many attractions during National Museum Weekend each April.

Ashford Castle

Ireland

Famously known as the Emerald Isle for its green, green pastures washed with abundant rain, Ireland is an unassuming jewel in the Atlantic Ocean. It's home to St Patrick, Guinness, the verbal felicity known as blarney, leprechauns (allegedly!) and a unique form of infectious humour and logic that encompasses every aspect of daily life. I've yet to meet a person who doesn't warm to the isle or its hospitable people.

Deep in the heartland of County Mayo near the western coast lies stately Ashford Castle, set against the sweeping backdrop of Lough Corrib and the rolling Connemara hills. Here in the wild countryside are echoes of our pre-historic past: the unique Céide Fields, with their buried remains of stone-walled fields, dwellings and tombs, dating back more than five thousand years. Ashford is a mere stripling in comparison, having been founded in 1228, but in its turn has grown into the landscape, with its lonely vantage point on the shoreline.

Originally built by the Anglo-Norman de Burgos family, following their defeat of the native O'Connors of Connaught, Ashford remained in the same clan for over 300 years. It passed into the hands of an Englishman, Lord Bingham, who added a fortified enclave within its precincts. By 1715 the estate was well established and owned by the Oranmore and Browne family, who added a fabulous French-style chateau wing to the castle. Contemporary history dates from 1852 when the new owner, Sir Benjamin Lee Guinness, extended the estate to 26,000 acres, including dozens of roads, literally millions of trees and shrubs and two huge Victorian extensions. The estate remained in the Guinness family until 1939 when Noël Huggard established it as a first-class hotel, set in 350 acres of its own private woodland.

Today's Ashford is owned by a group of Irish–American investors, who treasure its legacy with ardour and commitment.

As you approach the castle over the great cut stone bridge, the towering grey stone walls are imposing and initially quite intimidating, but in no time the warmth of the welcome

dispels any apprehensions. Entering the discreet stone portico, guests are escorted into the impressive George V Gallery, named after the then prince who was so enthralled with Ashford and its outstanding shooting that he extended his stay of two days to a month.

Huge picture windows in the sitting room overlook the formal garden designed by Arthur Sheketon, surrounded by expansive green lawns leading down to the lough.

Bedrooms stretch across the length and breadth of the castle, some with panoramic views of the lough, others overlooking the river and gardens. The most popular rooms are the spacious suites overlooking the lough – they demand that you take time to relax and experience the tranquillity induced by the stillness of the water. An eclectic mixture of furniture, paintings, four-posters, gleaming silver, and Waterford decanters filled with sherry all contribute to the quirky elegance and individualism of the rooms.

The Prince of Wales Cocktail Bar was specifically built for the visit of King George V

(opposite) **The Dungeon Bar.**   **Individually-styled bedrooms.**

– ideal for a cocktail or bar lunch. Afternoon tea is best enjoyed in the elegant drawing room sitting on one of the huge sofas over-looking the magnificent panoramic views of Lough Corrib. During the main season there's a choice of two restaurants: the George V Dining Room, offering classical Irish cuisine; or the Connaught Room, which offers a degustation menu of classical French cuisine. The Connaught Room's entrance is dominated by an impressive, hand-crafted, twenty-foot-high inglenook fireplace – a perfect spot for aperitifs or digestifs. Woodcarvings and delicate chateau-style furnishings combined with priceless oriental porcelain surround the tables. From the award-winning gourmet menu, guests often plump for the fresh fish caught in the lough that morning.

Following dinner, whether you're a coy recluse or a party reveller, you must visit the Dungeon Bar to join in a true Irish *craic*. The scene is set by the resident storyteller narrating tales of Irish folklore and myths, followed by nostalgic Irish tunes on the piano and great Irish harp accompanied by the stunning voice of Annette Griffin. It's commendable when general managers have the gumption to express the character of their hotel with unusual flair, and are prepared to take a risk by providing something out of the ordinary. A live sing-a-long in a five-star hotel is quite unimaginable anywhere else in the world – but in Ireland it's the very essence of local tradition and is much loved by everyone.

Ashford has welcomed its fair share of celebrities and public figures over the centuries. The Oscar-winning classic of the early 1950s, *The Quiet Man*, starring John Wayne and Maureen O'Hara, was filmed at Ashford and is still celebrated in the local pub – of the same name – to this day. Ashford's appeal appears universal: John Wayne to John Major, Bob Hope to Pierce Brosnan and Jane Seymour to Liam Gallagher, have all toasted the beauty of the Connemara while staying here.

Today's general manager, Niall Rochford, has a contagious passion for this part of Ireland and appears totally at home with guests of all ages. He's only too happy to accommodate with equal ease the needs of anyone from toddler to venerable aristocrat.

Ashford is full of outdoor adventures. For bicycle rides take a map of the estate marking the trails, appropriate pit stops and places of local interest, hop on and head off towards the lough. If something a little less energetic is called for, try the hour-long cruises on Lough Corrib, Ireland's second largest lake, on the *Lady Ardilaun*, including a visit to Inchagoill. One of the largest of the Lough Corrib Islands, you'll find two church ruins of immense historical interest here. Beside St Patrick's church is the Obelisk of Lugina,

Fly a hawk.   Horse and trap John Wayne style.   (opposite) **The Connaught Room.**

which marks the grave of St Patrick's nephew. The monumental stone carries – with the exception of the Roman Catacombs – the oldest Christian inscription in Europe.

Ashford's equestrian centre can organise a choice of rides through the charming wooded countryside between the shores of Lough Corrib and Lough Mask, and into the mountains of Connemara to the west – a stunning way to experience the local scenery.

For golfers the residential nine-hole course is irresistible. If you're not a golfer but take a good shot, the sporting clay range will test your skills against the bolting rabbit, springing teal or wily woodcock.

Lough Corrib is regarded as one of Europe's best salmon and brown trout fisheries. The lake is open to the public and a ghillie can be booked for a half or a full day's charter to increase your chances of a catch – mine was the one that got away!

If you've always wondered what it would be like to handle a bird of prey, then head straight to Ireland's School of Falconry on the estate – the 'Hawk Walks' are suitable for adults and children alike experiencing the rare thrill of flying a bird of prey at first hand. During an introductory lesson you will be taught how to handle and fly a Harris Hawk in the grounds of the Castle and watch a simulated hunt – unforgettable.

At the end of a vigorous day, you can be pampered in one of the health and beauty rooms or chill out in the health centre, which boasts computerised state-of-the-art fitness equipment, a whirlpool overlooking the lawns, steam room, sauna and relaxing conservatory fronting Lough Corrib. But whatever you do, make sure you leave enough time just to soak up the atmosphere and lull yourself into a blissful stupor, absorbing the natural beauty of an ageless landscape.

The Month
The mild climate and sparsely populated countryside of County Mayo make it ideal for hikers to enjoy the lush landscape as spring comes into bloom. April has the lowest rainfall of the year and offers some of the best fishing for salmon, bream and trout in the lough and nearby rivers.

Dhoni Mighili

Maldives

Have you ever dreamt of being whisked away to the perfect palm-fringed desert island surrounded by sparkling azure waters? If the answer is yes, then Dhoni Mighili in the Maldives is the ultimate nirvana for five-star Crusoe escapism.

The Maldivian archipelago is an extensive chain of twenty atolls lying off the southern tip of India and west of Sri Lanka. More than a thousand low-lying coral islands no taller than a palm tree above sea level plunge 4,000

metres into the ocean – a wonder of the world created over 50 million years ago when a line of volcanoes sank into the depths. Seen from an aeroplane, they look like droplets of turquoise tie-dye ink randomly speckled over the water.

The Maldivian reefs are home to thousands of fish and invertebrates including manta rays, moray eels, white tip reef sharks, barracuda, turtles, sea fans and brightly coloured corals. They're a magnet for humans too, in the shape of snorkellers and scuba fans.

Your arrival at Malé airport is an impressive portent of delights to come. The pier is literally steps away, and within minutes your privately owned *dhoni* – a hand-crafted, 65-foot yacht – sails around the corner to meet you. Where else in the world can you step off a plane into your bedroom? The four-hour journey to Mighili gives you the chance to shed your clothes and travel fatigue as Malé's silhouette disappears into a seamless ocean. For two hours you see nothing except an occasional dolphin or flying fish as you laze

on the deck. Just before tea the North Ari atoll appears under the low setting sun and the deep navy waters are again highlighted with glimmers of turquoise.

Unlike many of the hotels and resorts that advertise get-away-from-it-all peace, Dhoni Mighili is true liberation – no noisy boat traffic, no planes, no other tourists (apart from a maximum of ten other guests all seeking the same sanctuary) or any other jetsam and flotsam littering the horizon.

If that's not enough for you, what really makes it stand head and shoulders above the rest is the fact that it is the only resort that supplies its guests not just with the butler-fitted *dhoni* but also a sumptuous thatched 'beach shack'. It's akin to chartering a luxury yacht to explore the Med while simultaneously booking a suite at the Byblos just in case your sea legs fancy a rest.

Guests have a dedicated *thakuru* or butler who has the habit of appearing like a telepathic genie – your wish is his command throughout your stay, making your dreams a reality.

The *dhoni* bar.   The Spa   (opposite) The *dhoni* bedroom.

And that's what Dhoni Mighili is: a dream, cocooned from the cares of everyday life.

Each of the six *dhonis* has been masterfully fitted out with warm-toned Maldivian timber, a mixture of classical neutral eastern silks and Frette towels and linen. Shipshape here combines style with function. The avant-garde kitchen is equipped with up-to-the-minute appliances, including a pillar-box red SMEG fridge filled with frosted glasses, chilled Chablis and Tattinger. Philippe Starck accessories and bathroom fittings complete the furnishing, while shelves laden with L'Occitane de Provence toiletries promise pure pampering. Hidden in the dressing cabinet there's a sound system that will probably beat your one at home, a twenty-inch LCD screen with Bose DVD surround theatre, and a stack of selected CDs to suit your musical taste.

While you indulge in on-board hedonism, the Maldivian crew efficiently and unobtrusively handle the *dhoni*. Traditional

ivory-coloured sails hang on booms made from ancient banyan tree roots and are tied up with palm tree fronds. With one tug, all the fronds fly into the sea and the sails swell with the warm breeze.

If you'd rather sleep on terra firma, each of the six air-conditioned island bedrooms is fitted with the same comfortable king-size bed draped in Frette linen and down duvets – not that you'd ever get cold – lying below an intricately woven grass ceiling. Furniture has been kept to a minimum, with a long dressing table enclosing a mini bar with unusual midnight munchy treats such as Lavosh crisp-breads and quince and artichoke pastes.

Bathrooms are decorated in dark metallic shades of slate, and outdoors is brought indoors where the bath's shower attachment is held in place by a curving branch. A door leads out on to an enclosed courtyard with a tropical shower and plunge pool fed by a flowing wall of fresh water.

Notably, there's no television (unless you request one), as nothing should come between you and the soothing sound of the ocean as it drifts you into unconsciousness. The choice is yours – whether to sleep on your gently rocking *dhoni* or in your private beach abode.

Everywhere on this tiny island is barefoot paradise. Every floor, apart from the bedrooms and bathrooms, is made up of the finest silver sand particles found anywhere in the Maldives. The heart of activity revolves around the *dhoni*-shaped bar stocked with everything from amaretto to zambuca, with endless flowing Tattinger and a sublime selection of cocktails. Next to the bar a vertical wooden rowing boat filled with slats serves as a bookshelf and games cupboard.

Great care has been taken to offer something rather different on the menu at Mighili. There are no set meal times; you eat what, where and when you want. Hand-designed menus based on your preferences are collated

Dhoni sets sail.

daily and, if you love something the chef prepares for you at dinner, he'll be only too happy to share his secrets the next day and give you a private demonstration lesson.

No compromises have been made or standards spared for on-board dining. A picnic lunch here involves teak furniture (secretly boated on to your perfect uninhabited island while you are busy snorkelling round the reef) draped in crisp white linen, topped with frosted glasses, chilled wine and impossibly fresh tasting shellfish cooked on the BBQ by your butler, who'll even peel your prawns.

When it comes to spa treatments, there is none of the normal rush or compromise to ensure that you manage to fit your massage in. With a maximum of only twelve guests, both the treatment rooms (one in the open air where the sound of the waves will lull you into a feeling of calm and tranquillity) are readily available. A comprehensive menu of massage

therapies is expertly performed by amiable Thai girls trained to Chiva Som standards.

Maldivian people are natural hosts and immensely proud of their country. They love to see their guests happy and take personal care to ensure you enjoy their exquisite home. At Dhoni Mighili nothing appears too much trouble. Attentive care from Abcy, our gentle butler, and the charming New Zealand hosts Donna and Scott aimed for 100 per cent guest satisfaction – and succeeded.

All of this has been achieved as part of one man's vision for tourism in the Maldives. Managing director Tom McLoughlin has created an exquisitely indulgent format where you no longer have to gaze longingly across the ocean wondering what the island on the horizon holds – you can simply ask the captain to point your *dhoni* in that direction and explore. The hardest choice of the day is whether to be pampered on land or at sea.

To stay at Dhoni Mighili is quite simply to be a child again but in a grown-up body – for one week in your life, 'I want' translates into 'I get'.

Month
Average year-round temperatures range between 24° and 30°C (75°–86°F), and in general days are hot and humid. The Maldives are affected by seasonal monsoons: the north-east monsoon between November and April is hot and dry; while the south-west monsoon between May and October brings wind and rain. For divers, the best visibility is in March and April when the seas are calm and the skies are bluest. February and March are hot, but by April soothing breezes start to blow across the archipelago.

As Dhoni Mighili is a turtle-laying site you'll also have a chance to see turtles hatching if you time your stay during a full moon.

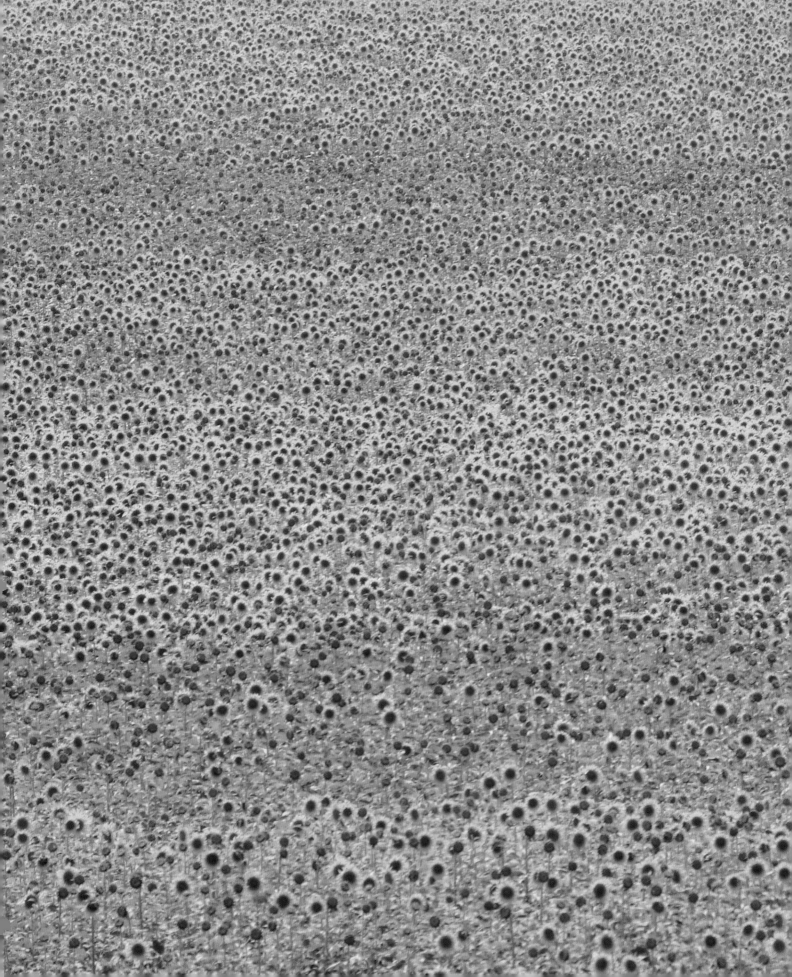

May

Amanjena

Marrakech

Founded in 1062 by the Amoravid Berbers from the Sahara as Morocco's second most important imperial city after Fez, Marrakech is not only the capital of the south but is recognised today as the country's flagship destination. Its lavish palaces and riads, thriving souks, hospitable people and lush palm, orange and olive groves all contribute to its popularity.

Today the city is divided into the *medina*, the old town, and the *gueliz*, the new town, built by the French during their occupation between 1912 and 1956. The *medina* is encircled by nineteen kilometres of impressive walls dating from the twelfth century standing nine metres high, punctuated by ten gates and over 200 towers. The main square, Place Jemaa el-Fna, is the very pulsating heart of the city and a riot of smell, sound and colour. At dusk, the square becomes the largest open-air dining room in Marrakech, serving among other traditional delicacies huge vats of snails marinated in cumin, lentils with mint and spicy *merguez*

sausages. Meanwhile, in this vibrant theatre of life, thousands gather in circles to be entertained by musicians, snake charmers, actors,comedians, and water-sellers who wear medieval costume and ring brass bells to announce their presence.

The hypnotic noise and congestion of the souks and Place Jemaa el-Fna are in stark contrast to the utter tranquillity of the Hotel Amanjena, which has been appropriately named, literally meaning 'peaceful paradise'. Situated seven kilometres outside Marrakech, surrounded by the Palmier – a huge expanse of palm trees – the views are dominated by the High Atlas Mountains.

A visit to the city ramparts and ancient Palais el-Badi makes it easy to trace the inspiration for architect Ed Tuttle's impressive design-plan for Amanjena. He perfectly depicts the finest Marrakechi tones, on a truly rousing scale, incorporating the timeless grandeur and calm of the once majestic palace. Furthermore, Amanjena's concentric layout and long serene reflection pools create a

soothing ambience of space and stillness.

As you enter through two huge intricately carved cedarwood doors-within-doors into the colonnade, the sound of overflowing water announces to your senses that you have arrived somewhere different – the atmosphere is a combination of regal palace and monastic minimalism. To the left lies the fumoir, furnished with cotton-covered banquettes, and to the right the elegant Moroccan restaurant adorned with over eighty onyx columns and *moucharabieh*-wood screens.

The thirty-four pavilion-style suites and six two-storey *maisons* surround a huge irrigation pool known simply as the *bassin*. Vast dome-shaped bedrooms are festooned with Berber rugs, cedarwood and suede furniture, surrounding an open log fire while a huge brass vase of over a hundred pink Marrakechi roses adorn the room. The king-size platform bed, dressed in cool linen sheets encasing a luxuriously snug cream mohair blanket, is butted by two impressive Moroccan ironwork lamps.

Dome-shaped bedroom. (opposite) **Marble soaking tub.**

Three sets of sliding doors lead out on to a garden courtyard characterised by the pillared *minzah* or gazebo dining area and a sofa for lounging, lit by candle lanterns and soothed by a gently trickling zellij-tiled fountain – made private by drawing the flowing cream drapes. The concentric pattern continues into the spacious bathroom, which has twin dressing rooms and washbasins opposite a stepped green Moroccan marble soaking tub.

The elegant swimming pool area is sheltered by an attractive hibiscus hedge and bordered on all sides by roofs lined in the same turquoise-green fish-scale-shaped zellij tiles, which perfectly complement the pink *pisé* stonework. During the hot summer months all meals are taken on the pool terrace where an extensive Moroccan, French and Thai à la carte menu is offered to the sound of live Moroccan music under clear starry skies.

The spa is appropriately dominated by two green-tiled *hammams* – Moroccan steam baths – complete with square Jacuzzi, and a gentle fountain surrounded by marble tables covered with glass jars of various coloured oils, candles and bowls of pale pink rose petals.

The signature treatment of the *hammam* is a central part of Moroccan life and not to be missed. It comprises a gentle steam bath and deep cleansing treatment to purify and soften the skin. After ten minutes sitting quietly on the green tiles, to open the pores, a bucket of hot water is douched over the entire body. Ebony-coloured olive soap is then smeared from head to toe and soothingly massaged in, followed by another douche. As you lie down on the green tiles, a black mitt, akin to a human scouring pad, is then rigorously rubbed up and down the length of your body, shedding staggering amounts of skin. Another douche is followed by a soothing layer of indigenous clay, lavender

kernels and ground rose petals mixed together in rose water, to calm and moisturise. A final hot douche followed by a cooler eucalyptus swash to seal and protect leaves a skin as soft as the proverbial baby's bottom. In Moroccan culture this cleansing ritual is carried out once a week for anyone from four months old – no wonder their skin has such radiance. You'll feel cleaner than you've ever felt in your life.

Other facilities include the adjoining golf course, hard-surface tennis courts, gym and a chic library well stocked with colourful books, CDs, videos and a selection of canvases for artists. In addition, a series of private excursions around Marrakech and the surrounding areas can be arranged, including trips into the High Atlas, Kasbah Telouet, country markets and the Nectarome – the only biological herb garden of North Africa, from where the bathroom toiletries are sourced.

(opposite) **Light and shade in the entrance collonade.** **The relaxing fumoir.** **Sunset at Amanjena.**

Exploring the narrow streets of the souks for colourful rugs, basketware, lamps, spices, leather and *babouche* slippers it is easy to get disorientated. The haggling banter of marketers is accompanied by the incessant noise of wheelbarrows being jerked along the cobbled paths, meowing cats, piercing bicycle bells, the clip-clop of donkeys' hooves as they pull their wooden carts and the flip-flop of *babouches* scurrying along. The game of bargaining is both expected and enjoyed, and so much more satisfying than a supermarket checkout.

For all that light-heartedness, a profound respect for tradition and values runs deep in the blood of the Moroccan people, strongly epitomised in the welcome received from any member of Amanjena's 200-plus staff, or

indeed in Marrakech itself. It is literally 'heart felt': a gentle bow of the head as the right hand reaches towards the heart, a greeting of '*As-salaam alaykum*' – 'Peace be upon you' – is as common as 'hello' elsewhere in the world.

After fifteen years with the Aman group, Ferdinand Worteboer, directeur général, has an integral understanding of culture and the reverence each race places upon the freedom to express their unique tastes and values. In a time when indigenous culture is often sanitised and homogenised, he finds the task of custodian of Morocco's finest hotel both challenging and exciting.

The Month

Morocco, the most western of all Arabic countries, is referred to by its inhabitants as

maghrib, or sunset. Bordered by the Atlantic and Mediterranean Seas to the north and west and the Atlas Mountains and Sahara dunes to the south, its subtropical location enjoys huge climatic diversity. Occasional rain falls between October and March, but the winters are generally temperate with average temperatures of 22°C (71°F). While you may not choose to visit the baking desert in May, Marrakech and the surrounding Atlas Mountains are most pleasant during this month with an average temperature of 27°C (81°F). The evenings and early mornings are clement enough for excursions and activities, and the afternoon heat is perfect for lazing by the pool. Although each room is air-conditioned, the cool fresh Atlas breezes are more than adequate for a good night's sleep.

Hacienda de San Rafael

Spain

Southern Spain is an area of striking contrasts. Just a stone's throw from Africa, it's well known for its flamboyant flamenco dancing, delicious tapas, sherry, Moorish architecture and bullfighting. All are never more evident than in the geographically diverse *comunidades autonomas* of Andalusia. The great fertile Andalusian plains lie to the north and west, as hills dotted with *pueblos blancos* (white villages) rise towards the Sierras to the east; and to the south you'll find the world's great sherry vineyards and the Atlantic beyond.

Located on a little knoll half-way between Seville and Jerez, there's a beautiful eighteenth-century estate – the Hacienda de San Rafael. Once a thriving olive farm, it embodies the traditional way of life in southern Spain. Set in 350 acres of its own farmland, it is part of the vast agricultural patchwork quenched by the Guadalquivir River. The surrounding plains are a spectrum of colour made up of rotating wheat, cotton, sugarbeet and dazzling sunflower crops.

A modest dusty drive in the middle of the plain, banked with rampant mounds of blossoming oleanders, leads up to the house – its whitewashed metre-thick walls smothered in a riot of bougainvillaea, jasmine and plumbago blooms.

In 1989 international hotelier Tim Reid and his Spanish wife Kuky, whose family have owned the estate for 140 years, rescued the hacienda from dereliction. Within three years the dilapidated building was totally regenerated and they decided to open the doors of their private hideaway. It was an instant coup. Their recipe for success combines informality backed up with total efficiency; guests feel utterly spoilt while completely at ease, as if they're staying in their own cosseted hideaway. As soon as you enter, you feel yourself relaxing into the peace and personal comfort of a home from home. Guests roam freely through the beamed drawing room, where the walls are decorated with stirrups belonging to Kuky's father, and the bright reading room,

which is scattered with ancient volumes and earthen vases filled with meadow flowers.

There is a choice of two different styles of bedroom. The bougainvillaea-filled courtyard acts as centre stage to eleven hacienda bedrooms, with a double bed or twin beds, each with a little sitting area and a pretty shaded veranda where breakfast is served each morning. Most have a wide arch leading to a bathroom with a bath and separate shower, and are charmingly decorated with hand-blocked cotton linens, family paintings, antique furniture and sheaves of fresh flowers from around the estate.

For something a little more special, treat yourself and stay in one of the three *casitas*, or split-level thatched cottages, on the southeast side of the hacienda building. Named 'Vanessa', 'Antonio' and 'Patricio', after Tim and Kuky's children, they are situated around a separate garden with their own private swimming pool. This is camouflaged from the house by towering mimosa, pepper and

Casa Vanessa and pool.   **Sombrajo.**

eucalyptus trees and high lavender bushes. Each is very private and has a large bedroom, separate living room and shaded *chozita* (or arbour) affording views towards the Sierras – an ideal spot for breakfast and lunch. All have attractive rose-hued adobe walls and herringboned terracotta floor tiles. Slate bathrooms have double vanities with Molton Brown toiletries, a bath, large slate-walled shower and a separate loo accessed via a rustic stable door. Each *casita* has a small pantry kitchen stocked with chilled wines, water, fruit and snacks, plus a galleried siesta zone. The eclectic mix of Spanish, English and Asian furniture, rugs, art, lamps and candles, make these little houses irresistible.

Around the pool the flourishingly dense lawns that put a spring in your step are interspersed with rustic straw parasols shading cushioned bamboo sun loungers. Throughout the day you'll be entertained by the acrobatic swallows that dart and dive to drink from the pool then soar into the air. Indeed, the bird life is one of the major

attractions of the hacienda as each February thousands of birds migrate from Africa to the cooler climes of southern Europe. Within the grounds, resident goldfinches gorge themselves on the pervasive thistles alongside crested larks and ubiquitous long-beaked bee-eaters.

While there's no obligation to dine in-house, it would be a mistake to miss the hacienda's marvellous cooking. Whenever possible, eating takes place outside. Each morning starts with a continental breakfast of freshly squeezed Seville orange juice, aromatic Saimaza coffee, croissant and home-made *pan*, *bollos* and *tortas* with jam, served on your veranda or in the peaceful shade of your *chozita*. Most guests eat out for lunch but there is a basic à la carte lunch menu, best enjoyed in the gardens by the pool. At dinner-time everyone comes together in an informal house-party way, gathering around the sunset bar by the poolside.

During the day the chef visits guests to discuss the evening's three-course dinner

menu and selected wines. Menus are deftly based on fresh local products in season. Good simple flavours are brought out with the natural help of olive oil, onions, garlic, herbs, and of course the locally made sherry. Local chefs vow that sherry is the world's most valuable liquid asset, forever adding a blast of flavour and transforming an otherwise unremarkable dish into something quite delectable.

No two evenings are likely to be the same as guests have a choice of at least three different open-air dining venues. The *sombrajo*, or thatched dining area in the family's private Eastside Garden, is regularly converted into a fragrant dining area, surrounded by citrus trees and strongly scented flowers and herbs. The bougainvillaea-filled central courtyard is picture-postcard pretty, so it makes perfect sense to be able to enjoy it at leisure over a meal – and it has one other unique feature. At about ten o'clock each night flocks of flamingos fly directly overhead from the feeding grounds of the Donana national park back to their nesting grounds around the lakes. They make

Casa Patricio living room.   **Courtyard bedroom.**   (opposite) **Casa Antonio bedroom.**

the hundred-mile round trip at the same time each day, to the extent that locals will set their watches by the astonishing sight.

Tim and Kuky's charming son Anthony has recently taken over the day-to-day management of the estate. It must have been an easy decision – he's as committed as his parents with an easy charisma so suited to his role, and utterly passionate about Spain. His contagious enthusiasm for the local region and vision for future development will undoubtedly secure this owner-run hideaway for another generation to come.

As you would expect, being outside is the fundamental pleasure of San Rafael. As well as the gorgeous garden spilling over with plants around the three swimming pools, there's a 'paddle' tennis court on the sheltered west side offering an amusing way to warm up for that apéritif.

No one would blame you for disappearing and passing a lazy day in one of the cosy corners around the property – but dozens of local attractions await if you're feeling adventurous.

In the surrounding area are numerous picturesque *pueblos blancos*, and, high up in the Sierras, along the old *bandito* routes, the famous griffin vultures can be spotted gliding high with the thermals then swooping down into the gorge. Few people go there, but those who do will savour the unpolluted air and the distinctive smell of the living earth. Jerez's renowned horses and sherry bodegas are under an hour away and Seville's Alcázar and Giralda cathedral are a must-see.

Authentic Spanish life is best experienced in the market towns between nine o'clock and noon, where a tangible excitement infuses the very air. Wander among the market stalls and you may be lucky enough to see a burst of spontaneous Jerezana life: for no apparent reason a crowd will suddenly beat out a rhythm with clapping hands, as men goad each other on into an electrifying dance. They hold their audience spellbound for a while, but then the spectacle finishes as quickly as it starts – like a sharp echo of ancestral energy.

The Month

Spring comes early in Andalusia, where the countryside's colours are most dramatic during harvesting at the end of May. Among the grazing bulls, swathes of wild flowers stretch from the path-side up into the Sierras as a sweeping mauve wave of Michaelmas daisies, poppies and orchids. In May the fields surrounding the hacienda are fertile green with a blast of yellow as sunflowers turn their heads to follow the sun. From mid-June the colours metamorphose as everything starts to burn under the intense summer sun – the ground turns black and only the hardy olive trees are resistant. May days are comfortably hot and nights are still cool enough to need a blanket.

Twenty-five minutes by car, Jerez's annual *feria* takes place, always in May (four weeks after Easter). Roads are covered in compacted intense golden *albero* earth acting like a yellow brick road for every man and his horse going to the fair, with particular excitement on Wednesday and Thursday – bullfight nights.

Ananda Spa

India

Nestled in a hundred acres of the Himalayan foothills, the world-class destination spa of Ananda is dedicated to travellers looking for innovative ways to rejuvenate themselves. It lies in the state of Uttaranchal, some 260 kilometres north of New Delhi in a small town called Narendra Nagar. Located in the grounds of the palace estate of the Maharaja of Tehri-Garhwal, you'll find the holy town of Rishikesh close by.

It is best reached by the four-hour journey on Indian Railways' comfortable Dehradun Shatabdi Express, across India's raw natural landscape. At Haridwar station you then take an hour's drive, passing through Rishikesh and along the intriguing ridges and valleys of the Himalayas.

It is said that the Pandavas took the final walk of their lives ascending the slopes of a peak in western Garhwal called 'Swagaronhini' – literally translated as 'the ascent to heaven'. No one can say for sure whether or not the Ananda spa is built on the very spot referred to, but all its guests agree that the view over-looking the Ganges valley is a breathtaking visual paradise.

The palace was originally built as a mountain residence for the Maharaja, who wished to escape the stifling heat of the Indian summer. In 1910 an annexe was added to commemorate the arrival of the British Viceroy and his entourage, and it is currently the point of welcome for today's guests.

Concealed by the resplendent palace lies the faded elegance of the Art Deco reception area, where guests are greeted and presented with a necklace of Rudraksha beads, known by locals as 'the tears of Lord Shiva' and believed to hold powers of healing and relaxation. Guests are led through to the Viceregal Tea Lounge – a room of old-world charm decorated in shades of yellow and blue, believed to be the colours of royalty. You'll also find life-size portraits of the Maharaja, and famous guests including the last Viceroy of India, Lord Mountbatten, and Indira Gandhi.

Ananda's main spa and accommodation are located further down the hill in an array of newly created pavilion-style buildings positioned on a foothill ridge. Make sure you request one of the seventy-five rooms and suites that have a celestial view overlooking the holy Ganges River and valley of Rishikesh far below. At dawn the rooms are infused with pure Himalayan light, imbibing the majesty of the mountains – enticing you outside for some spontaneous meditation. The fresh mountain air and a steaming mug of ginger and lemon tea to invigorate the body and mind are the standard start to every day.

Bedrooms have been designed in a minimalist and holistic fashion, with wooden floors and simple furniture covered with natural fabric. The walk-in closet holds a supply of the optional spa attire of freshly pressed white linen 'kurta pyjama' shirts and trousers, which is regularly replenished.'

Well-lit marble bathrooms with a shower as well as a sunken bath face the exquisite panorama, and are the model setting for a deliciously scented rose-petal bath to soothe away your journey. Next to the bath, herbal

The Music Pavilion.   Shirodhara.   (opposite) **Ganges View.**

distillates, essential oils, plant extracts, crushed flowers, roots and barks have been blended together to create various tonics for you to use.

Most people visit Ananda for two things – the spa and the yoga. One huge advantage over other spas is the daily programme of complimentary activities including yoga, dance, trekking and cooking demonstrations. The ultimate spa nirvana, Ananda offers a blend of therapeutic treatments based on the traditional Indian practices of Ayurveda, yoga and meditation as well as the latest European and Thai treatments that promise to purify the body and soothe the senses. An impressive array of sixteen treatment rooms, four relaxation rooms and four consultation rooms are split into four areas: Ayurvedic, European, yoga and fitness.

Many massages are carried out on indigenous jackfruit-wood tables and each treatment begins with a distinctive chant of 'shanti, shanti, shanti' as your feet are

cleansed in rose-petal water and your head is anointed with warm oil. Massages vary from gentle strokes to vigorous head-to-toe rubs designed to increase circulation and detoxify, leaving you feeling utterly relaxed.

Facilities include a separate beauty treatment salon and a Kama Suite for couples with a private aromatherapy bath. Men's and women's complete hydrotherapy facilities include a Turkish steam room; a Finnish sauna and whirlpool overlooking the valley; a Kneipe foot bath of naturally rounded Ganga pebbles; and a chilling plunge pool. In addition there are two squash courts, a six-hole golf course, an outdoor pool and Jacuzzi, a sixteen-station gymnasium for cardio and strength training, and aerobics facilities.

This region of the Himalayas is the birthplace of Ayurveda, the holistic system of healing encompassing diet, massage, exercise and yoga. It uses an analytical process to identify the imbalance in the body's three main bio energies or doshas called Vata, Pitta

and Kapha. For centuries native people have corrected the balance with herbs sourced from the natural wealth of the forest foothills to achieve health and harmony. A consultation

(opposite) **Spa Reception.** **Spa cuisine.**

with the in-house doctor will diagnose your dosha type and create a personalised therapy and activity programme in the areas of stress, detoxification, relaxation, anti-ageing and weight loss, while offering guidance on nutrition and exercise.

Today, yoga enjoys global popularity. Devotees believe that it helps to achieve a state of passive alertness that transcends the normal everyday level of thought and distraction. At Ananda the yoga programme is designed to enhance physical, mental, emotional and spiritual well-being using three branches: Hatha, Kriya and Raja. Resident instructors customise one-hour sessions around the simple movements of the Asana (postures), Mudras (gestures), Pranayama (deep breathing) and Dhyana (meditation). The backdrop of the

Himalayan sal forest and the stunning open-air pavilion, surrounded by a channel of still water, makes it an enviable location for any exercise and the perfect spot for the dusk Sadana classes, which focus on Pranayama, Asana and Dhyana.

In western cultures, a healthy diet is thought to be a balance of macro-nutrients such as proteins and carbohydrates, whereas many eastern cultures believe we should satisfy our food cravings by paying attention to six contrasting flavours. These are sweet, sour, salty, astringent, bitter and pungent – and the Ayurvedic diet is totally orientated to satisfy this nutrient-rich regime. Food forms a quintessential element of Ananda philosophy and is an integral part of rejuvenation. The spa's basic guiding principle is that it should not be

thought of as a place to diet or lose weight but should instead introduce a 'way of life'. The approach is a healthier alternative to regular meals without having to go hungry, incorporating a foundation of low-calorie, high-nutrition meals, which are exotically flavoured and aesthetically pleasing.

Built in a picturesque grove of old sal trees, overlooking the valley of Rishikesh, The Restaurant offers a spa cuisine menu highlighting the philosophy of better living, by providing food enriched with the natural flavour of organic vegetables and herbs. Ananda's objective is to offer a cuisine that rejuvenates guests who desire to revitalise their bodies and minds through a healthy approach to diet and lifestyle.

Outside the estate there's plenty to explore.

Ampitheatre.   (opposite) **Aarti in Rishikesh.**

Nearby Rishikesh is recognised as the yoga capital of the world and the birthplace of Ayurveda. Thousands of pilgrims flock to bathe in the sacred Ganges, and the ashrams at Rishikesh are famous for their daily evening ritual of the 'Ganga Aarti' – an auspicious Hindu ritual performed on the banks of the river. Since time immemorial, the holy source has been worshipped and propitiated for the bounty and prosperity showered on the Gangetic Plains.

The Aarti ceremony provides a spectacular visual joy and a sublime and unforgettable spiritual experience. The one-and-a-half-hour ritual starts with the Yagna, an offering of herbs and clarified butter on a fire to purify the surrounding environment and to invite the holy vibrations. Young boys with shaven heads dressed in orange robes bow towards the sacred river to the sounds of chanting prayer accompanied by cymbals, drums, horns and bells as wafts of smoke disappear into the skies. At twilight, considered in Indian philosophy as the most auspicious

moment of the day, thousands of earthen diyas (lamps) are set afloat on the Ganges: an act of reverence to the holy river. With the scent of sandalwood incense and the melodious chants of the holy priests, the Ganga Aarti is undoubtedly the most soul-stirring act of reverence and prayer.

Fourteen kilometres north of Ananda the highest peak in the immediate area, known as Kunjapuri, soars more than 1,500 metres. It is crowned with one of twelve sacred shrines commemorating the goddess Shakti, the consort of Lord Shiva. The trek to the snow-capped Himalayas, passing ubiquitous wild sage, thyme and ginger, is best enjoyed at sunrise or sunset when the daily rituals take place. Guided by the spa staff, the four-hour trek takes you back in time, passing paddy-fields with smiling curious children tending their sheep, and simple farmhouse roofs covered in drying corn kernels. At the summit the final climb up a flight of 308 steps rewards you with a breathtaking panoramic view – it's well worth the effort.

Whether it's physical, mental or spiritual rejuvenation you're seeking, Ananda's exceptional spa facilities are situated in one of the most beautiful corners of the earth. A trip to the birthplace of yoga, Ayurveda and meditation will go a long way to restoring a healthy equilibrium, and you will return home with a greater sense of wellbeing – so much so that you will want to return again the same time every year.

The Month

While May is too hot and steamy for most of India, it's the perfect time of year to enjoy the warm days and cool nights in elevated Narendra Nagar, which has a moderate climate throughout the year. Ambient temperatures are pleasant all year except during a brief period in winter (December and January) when it drops to a cool 6°C (43°F) at night. At an altitude of 1,000 metres, the invigorating ozone-rich air is noticeably pure, and deliciously perfumed by the wild-flower blossoms of springtime.

June

Hotel Ritz

Madrid

Europe's fourth largest city, Madrid, is renowned for its vital nightlife and football, but mainly for its architecture, reflecting a range of artistic periods that have defined the city throughout the centuries. Its name originates from the Arabic fortress *Magerit* or 'mother of the waters', on the bank of the Manzanares River, and although it expanded under a prosperous Arab regime for more than two hundred years, very little remains of their presence. Most of the city's great monuments are in an area referred to as the Madrid de los Austrias, a splendid collection of rather austere seventeenth-century baroque-style façades with lavish interiors.

The Hotel Ritz occupies the most coveted location in Madrid, right in the cultural heart of the historic hub beside the Prado Museum and close to the Royal Palace. The botanical gardens and the Parque del Retiro are also nearby, with the parliament and stock exchange only a stroll away. A stellar example of the Belle Epoque era, the hotel was built as one of the original grand luxury hotels of Europe.

Madrid had always been a city of intense vitality, noble buildings, wide and sparkling plazas and exquisite gardens, but, early in the twentieth century, the young Spanish king, Alfonso XIII, had new ideas for his capital. He had been travelling in Europe, where he had been royally entertained, and he returned home with memories of splendid palaces, state rooms, parks and fountains. He was the first to realise how much his capital city would gain by the addition of a hotel of the same calibre as the Ritz in Paris – a hotel to satisfy the tastes of the most distinguished and discerning among a new type of traveller, only just beginning to be called tourists.

The king's inspiration became a reality, and the hotel was designed and built under the personal supervision of legendary hotelier César Ritz. Since its opening in 1910, its history has reflected that of Spain: its salons, terraces and gardens seeing a steady stream of kings and aristocrats, prime ministers, diplomats, generals and artists.

The 137 rooms and thirty suites all overlook the hotel garden, the Lealtad Square or the Prado Museum, and are lavishly decorated in rich Mediterranean tones. Fine upholstered furniture, locally hand-stitched carpets from the Real Fábrica de Tapices, embroidered linen sheets, and luxurious marble bathrooms complete the look. The hotel also has a well-equipped fitness centre, sauna, massage, solarium, hair salon and beauty centre to meet every pampering desire.

Like most cities, Madrid has always had a magnetic effect on its surrounding regions. Over the years it has become a melting pot of people, cultures and, most emphatically, its very own Madrileño gastronomy. As such, it is a natural home to the tapas bar, where dozens of small saucers of food are lined up side by side to accompany a glass of wine or sherry. Madrid is the unchallenged tapas capital of the world, with excellent seafood, Iberian ham, sausages, pickles and native dishes such as prawns in batter and Madrid-style tripe or snails. You'll also find countless smoked

Deluxe Suite. Terrace.

meats, excellent sheep's cheese, casseroles, and all kinds of local wines.

Within the hotel, the highly acclaimed Goya restaurant offers a mouth-watering menu of local Spanish specialities as well as a comprehensive international cuisine. A special Sunday brunch is best taken on the elegant terrace overlooking the garden, where white wicker armchairs and marble tables covered with crisp linen tablecloths provide a relaxing summer setting. The grand Lobby Bar serves traditional afternoon tea and light refreshments, to the delightful background of harp, piano or classical Spanish guitar.

Start your evening in the intimate Velázquez Bar, a popular rendezvous for Madrileños who gather for a drink before heading out for a night of partying. On the whole, life in Spain remains very traditional and continues to centre on strong family values and customs – which do not get in the way of enjoying life to the full. Night time has an energy all of its own, especially from Thursday to Saturday, when tapas bars and nightclubs usually stay open until dawn. Because of the intense midday heat, many people will still take a traditional siesta during the day. The evening begins with *el paseo*, a leisurely stroll through the main streets to show off immaculately dressed children, followed by an early tapas to keep going, and most won't sit down for dinner before ten o'clock.

(opposite) **Main entrance.**   **Palacio de Cristal.**   **Early evening tapas.**

When the rest of Europe is climbing into bed, the Madrid nightlife is only just warming up.

Within easy reach of the Ritz there are any number of attractions. The 2,000-roomed Royal Palace, with its magnificent reception rooms and state apartments, is particularly worth a visit. The city's real artistic wealth is found in its galleries. Pride of place belongs to the well-known Paseo del Arte, which is actually made up of a 'golden triangle' of three remarkable museums, situated very close to one another: the Prado (considered by many experts to be the best art gallery in the world), the Thyssen Bornemisza, and the Queen Sofía National Art Centre. Alternatively, you could visit the Monasterio de las Descalzas Reales, founded by the widowed Queen of Portugal in 1557, a convent of barefoot Franciscan nuns containing many rare

treasures and one of the most beautiful squares in Madrid. For more worldly pursuits, there's a plethora of top designer shops based along Calle Ortega y Gasset, but if you're shopping for leather or Catalonian textiles, try the half open, half galleried, Rastro market on a Sunday morning. There, the local hustle and bustle is at its most vibrant and a walk or boat ride in Retiro Park afterwards makes a perfect day out.

The Month

The region of Madrid generally has a semi-arid Mediterranean climate, with noticeable climatic extremes produced by its central geographical position and high altitude. Winters tend to be cold and the summers very hot. Thanks to *My Fair Lady*, it's well known that 'the rain in Spain falls mainly on the

plain' – it's less well known that most of it falls in spring. By June, the skies are clear and humidity is at its lowest – perfect for sight-seeing and partying al fresco.

Hotel Eisenhut

Germany

Lying on the northern tip of rural Bavaria, the walled town of Rothenburg is regarded by many as the epitome of medieval Germany. Reminiscent of Italy's Lucca, the town stands proud as a treasured relic of life in the Middle Ages with its cobbled streets, fortified towers and painted façades. Entering is like stepping into a historical picture book come to life.

Like most European settlements, its fortunes have fluctuated over the centuries. In 1274 it became a 'free city' of the Holy Roman Empire under special protection of the Emperor – a privilege that initiated great prosperity. It developed into a major trading centre supporting a population of over 6,000 – huge for its day. Once developed, the town represented a major crossroads for merchants and a welcome stop for those travelling the latitudinal trail from Prague to Paris and longitudinal route from Scandinavia to Italy.

The town was eventually crippled by a succession of disastrous wars, and left to rot for centuries, until the romantic period of German art in the mid-nineteenth century breathed new life into the beleaguered walls. Droves of artists and poets flocked to the town, creating something of a mecca.

Its medieval architecture remains largely intact. Each building has a prominent hoist jutting out from its gable – a relic of medieval uncertainty when households were required by law to store enough grain in their lofts to feed their inhabitants for a year in case of siege. Entrances remain wide enough for a horse and carriage to pass, but thankfully the days of hurling the contents of chamber pots onto the streets below have long since passed.

Since the Middle Ages Herrngasse has been the town's most eminent street. Houses that line the pavements around the square were built by the richest and most powerful families of the region. Today, four of these sixteenth-century patrician houses – the main three on one side of the street, an additional bedroom annexe directly opposite – form the Hotel Eisenhut. Guests enter through the doors of the oldest house into a beamed reception hall, converted from an ancient chapel complete with Gothic iron doors, arched passageways and solid stone pillars. It was here that George Eisenhut started a small inn in 1876, selling local wines cultivated in the Tauber Valley. On his death he passed the inn to his son-in-law Johann Ploss, the great-grandfather of the current owner, Dr Hans Pirner.

Throughout the hotel, oak floorboards are covered with antique Persian rugs, while ancient tapestries line the walls of the halls alongside stone and oak pillars covered in axes, shields and terrifying weapons of mass destruction belonging to the seventeenth and eighteenth centuries. Deep coffers and ticking grandfather clocks stand where they were originally placed on long Persian runners.

The sounds of church bells and birds awaken you each morning. From the back of the hotel are stunning views across the ramparts towards the valley, and to the front, lines of grand houses flank the street. Outside is a pretty 'beer garden' terrace leading down through vineyards to the valley.

(opposite) **Small dining room.**   Rothenburg.   **Topplerschloesschen.**

Hotels across rural Germany demonstrate a quirky quality in interiors, and are quite different from the rest of Europe in style and taste. Here, the eclectic mix of spinning wheels, Venetian mirrors, iconic statues and waist-high doors lends the buildings an air of timelessness. Some bedrooms are decorated with antique beds and furniture, while others have a distinctive 1970s feel with an idiosyncratic combination of patterned carpets and floral wallpaper – something of a time warp. All the bedrooms have en suite facilities, two with whirlpool baths and one with a mosaic wall and marble bath.

After a day sightseeing, you can enjoy a glass of the local bubbly at the bar. The collage of sketches and watercolours above the leather corner seat were gifts from previous guests wanting to express their appreciation in something more demonstrative than the visitors' book. At night olden tunes such as

Fur Elise resonate from the grand piano as guests enter the dining room. A huge painting depicts the legendary Master Draught and the tale of Mayor Nusch, who is said to have saved the town from occupation by General Tilly during the Thirty Years War. Each Whitsun the scene is re-enacted by hundreds of locals dressed in costume to celebrate the triumph, culminating in a grand parade.

The hotel is entitled to be proud of its excellent cuisine. Specialities include roasted fillet of pike, followed by a knuckle of veal with an unusual and delicious tureen of bread. Puddings are always colourful and include delicate flavours such as a cream of woodruff with a strawberry salad. You'll see a delicious local delicacy in dozens of shop windows around the town – *schneeballen* are balls of biscuits dusted to look like snowballs and flavoured with chocolate, marzipan and various icings.

Having remained in the same family for generations, the Eisenhut has an air of domestic stability. Staff treat you as a friend of the family and genuinely care about the quality of service provided. Assistant general manager Frank Schimmer has an impressive attitude towards the needs of his guests, and takes a personal pride in your comfort.

Main dining room. **Four poster.** (opposite) **Hallway.**

Outside the hotel there's much to see. Accompanying the town's night watchman on his evening rounds is an experience not to be missed, and is best taken on your first night so you can orientate yourself through the myriad sights and sounds. At eight o'clock, crowds congregate opposite the town hall and wait for the clock on the tower to strike. The windows open and wonderful painted figures appear from the windows – rather like a giant cuckoo clock.

The watchman brings the town's unique medieval heritage to life with tales of woe and delight in equal measure, as he leads dozens through the cobbled alleyways like a modern-day Pied Piper. Traditionally the grave digger and executioner shared the job, passing through the streets with a halberd, a threatening axe-like weapon, as they lit the lamps and locked the gates. The tradition continued until 1920 when electric lamps were introduced.

Towns were often saved by their fortifications and Rothenburg was no exception – amazingly it is still surrounded by a timber-roofed wall interspersed with six gate towers. The hundreds of named plaques along the ramparts are a record of the people who sent money to rebuild the town after the Second World War.

A walk through the lush Tauber Valley is a delightful way to spend an afternoon. Better still, pack a picnic and wander down to the pretty meadow by the curious Topplerschloeschen, built in 1388 for the mayor who used it as his summer residence.

Strong nerves are required for a visit to the Medieval Crime Museum, which holds a macabre collection of instruments used for torture and punishment. Those with a more gentle disposition are better off at the Doll and

Toy Museum, packed to the rafters with thousands of dolls from across the globe. If you're in the mood for a festive extravaganza, the Christmas Museum, open all year round, is full of colourful trinkets and decorations, while those wanting to learn more about Rothenburg should visit the Reichsstadtmuseum for the town's history.

You may be fortunate enough to see the black-clad chimney-sweep strolling down the street – locals say that if he appears from your left you'll receive some good luck... which hopefully will bring you back to this romantic and enchanting town.

The Month

In June the town holds its annual music festival in the balmy summer air, a popular event attracting thousands. As you walk around the cobbled streets the coo of pigeons is never far away; many buildings are smothered in wisteria blooms while small garden plots, viewed from the wall, are flourishing. If June isn't possible, visit in December for the Christmas Fair or in September when thousands gather for the Imperial City Festival, when 700 years of history are spectacularly re-enacted throughout the streets culminating in a giant firework display.

Bovey Castle

England

In the beautiful English county of Devon, deep in the moorlands of Dartmoor, lies an undulating vale just south of the picturesque village of North Bovey – a quintessentially English parish filled with chocolate-box thatched cottages, a pretty church and cosy pub. At the brow of the hill rests an elegant baronial pile of sandy-grey stone with lofty picture windows, stone balconies and porticoes, blending into the fell.

Bovey Castle is the latest venture of international entrepreneur Peter de Savary. Over the last twenty-five years he has been creating what he describes as lifestyle-orientated clubs and hotels with a strong bias towards his favourite leisure pursuits and golf courses. After his huge success with Skibo in Scotland, he has once again excelled himself.

The Castle sits in 500 acres of parkland, formal gardens and rivers set within 368 square miles of Dartmoor's National Park, only half an hour's drive from the coast's sandy beaches. Throughout the estate exten-sive herbaceous borders have been restored in keeping with the style of traditional Victorian gardens at the turn of the last century. At every viewpoint eyes are drawn to follies, lakes, secluded thatched pavilions, ornamental garden furniture and the pretty bubbling River Bovey.

The building itself exudes the impression of being much older than its youthful century – it was originally built in 1906 by Viscount Hambledon, the son of the business baron W.H. Smith. He spared no expense in crafts-manship or scale when he transformed it in the 1920s, creating a country seat complete with panelled oak rooms, grand fireplaces and ornate Adam ceilings.

You enter through the main gate on to a red gravelled driveway, flanked by several of the celebrated golf links, which guides you to an imposing bank of crenellated stone and two giant mythological-looking sparrowhawks. The welly-boot-littered entrance hall leads directly into the central reception space, known as the Cathedral Room due to its impressive vaulted oak beams, a stunning 30-foot-tall stone fireplace, and an intricately carved minstrels' gallery.

Ground-floor rooms, opening on to the south-facing balustraded garden terraces, have been faithfully restored in theatrical Art Deco style. Leading from the long Great Hall are several bright airy sitting rooms, a library complete with sturdy carved elephant seats grouped around a chess board (plus some chirping canaries!), a billiard room, and an inviting bar with comfortable green leather Chesterfield sofas. The hall's ruby-red wall-to-wall carpeting absorbs most of the passing clamour, and little nooks and crannies are filled with comfy sofas and tables festooned with orchids, glossy magazines and news-papers, while the working organ and large rocking horse prove irresistible to children. All in all, the choice and variety of rooms have created a congenial club atmosphere where guests are free to mingle or hide away, just as they please.

Suite. (opposite) **Cathedral Room fireplace.**

Outside the Piano Bar, a discreet Internet point has been ingeniously concealed in an old oak telephone booth. The bar contains a choice of over 150 cocktails; most popular of which is a delicious new concoction appropriately named a De Savary Affair – a mixture of champagne, grapefruit and peach juice. Before dinner it's well worth visiting the cellar for the daily tasting with knowledgeable sommelier John Jardine, who will guide you through the eclectic mix of Old and New World wines to make a suitable selection to accompany your dinner.

Intricate hand-coloured chinoiserie silk wall paintings decorate the castle's striking main restaurant – the elegant 1920s Palm Court. Tables are draped in starched white linen with lacquered decoupage cloches and specially commissioned engraved glasses designed by Paloma Picasso: the result is pure theatre. Thankfully, the menu lives up to its surroundings and a four or five-course dinner is served every night, including such

culinary delights such as braised oxtail tartlet with parsnip puree followed by poached pears in an aniseed cornet and liquorice ice cream.

Upstairs, most of the sixty-five bedrooms have spectacular views over the valley's patchwork of fields and streams. The informal Deco theme continues throughout, with simple stylish colour schemes, upholstered chairs, 1920s Vogue prints and furniture on classic Edwardian lines. Bathrooms have been designed in an inventive interpretation of what could be twenty-first-century Art Deco, with zebra print wall coverings, black ceilings, monochrome prints and plenty of glass and chrome displaying ornamental orchids and fragrant Essential Elements toiletries.

The west wing of the castle houses a gymnasium and swimming pool in the Orangery, opening on to a sun terrace with stunning far-reaching views, while the state-of-the-art spa offers an extensive menu of health and Clarins beauty treatments that leave you feeling brand new.

Staff have been carefully recruited in every department, and express a subtle confident pleasure in their service. De Savary has an incredible flair for picking a team, and many of his core troupe are loyal employees from his other establishments around the world who have followed him to Devon. In particular the castle is lucky to have Club Director Henrietta Fergusson, who endeavours to make every guest's visit unforgettable – for all the right reasons. It's the little things that often make the difference, like being offered a tour in one of the Castle's vintage cars because it needs a run. The staff at Bovey are full of fun ideas that are both novel and seemingly effortless.

Each morning a list of activities is displayed next to reception, with details of the daily falconry display, egg collecting, fly-fishing, archery, shooting lessons, walks, adventures and tours arranged by the charming Estate Manager, Freddie Cartwright. If none of that appeals, you can opt for tennis, croquet,

(opposite) **Fly fishing on the River Bovey.**   **North Lodge suite.**

badminton or boules or the more unusual pastimes of bee keeping, fudge making, basketry and apple pressing. And for the more adventurous there's potholing, rock climbing, abseiling and canoeing, or less vigorous lessons in bird song, bridge, astrology, piano, gardening or cookery.

No one would blame you for not leaving the castle grounds, but there's plenty to do and see beyond the estate. The walk to the local pub is a gentle meander along the bubbling River Bovey, crossing an ancient stone bridge and pretty whitewashed cottages. You'll almost definitely see deer and possibly a heron or two. Further afield the castle has its own classic Riva launch for picnic boat trips from Dartmouth to Totnes on the scenic River Dart. The Castle also owns an equestrian centre offering lessons and hacks across the moors for all levels of experience.

For angling enthusiasts, the estate owns eleven miles of exceptional fishing for trout and salmon along the Rivers Bovey and Teign.

Set within the National Park, the rivers are bordered by steep valleys, characteristic granite outcrops and dramatic scenery with plentiful wildlife.

Golfers swoon over the Old Course at Bovey Castle – a challenging and beautiful championship golf course designed in 1926 by J.F. Abercromby, one of the finest British golf course designers of the Golden Era.

Children are more than welcome at Bovey and will be head over heels at the abundance of activities offered to them, including treasure and scavenger hunts, a woodland adventure site, dam building, trampolining, fly fishing, kite flying and a private cinema complete with fizzy drinks and popcorn. Mealtimes are specially arranged to fit round their needs, while maintaining the status quo for unaccompanied adults, and several bedrooms have been specifically designed complete with toys and are guaranteed to delight.

All the staff at Bovey Castle wear a special badge in the shape of the fairy-tale 'Devon

Chough' (half bird and half fish), a symbol of the valley's enchanted character. As a guest in this sophisticated corner of Devon you too can enjoy the best of both worlds and feel at home in your Barbour by day and Prada by night. Bovey was meant to be de Savary's swansong, but I have a feeling that he won't stop here – meanwhile, Devon is certainly Heaven.

The Month

The warmer climes of June see the start of the West Country's main cultural summer events, including bread weighing at Ashburton, the Goose Fair at Tavistock, the Town Criers' Championship at Newton Abbott, the Two Moors Festival and so much more. It's also the perfect month to visit the nearby Eden Project, a massive biodome complex of important and entertaining ecological discovery. Dozens of events at National Trust properties and the county's annual agricultural show take place in June each year, attracting visitors from all over the country.

July

Four Seasons Hotel George V

Paris

I love Paris. Every time I set foot on its streets my heart leaps at the prospect of discovering more of the treasures within France's capital of style and glamour. The millions who are drawn to Europe's most romantic city will tell you that it begs to be explored on foot, as its compact layout means everything lies within easy walking distance. While small on a city scale, it's so well laid out that there is always a feeling of spaciousness.

Broad tree-lined cobbled avenues flanked with shuttered houses are interspersed with lavish formal gardens, and at the heart of the city La Seine meanders its way through like a flowing silver ribbon. Whether you come for the architecture – classic or avant-garde – the peerless food or the rich and varied culture, the experience will exceed all your expectations.

Situated just off the Champs-Elysées, on a grand tree-lined boulevard, the Four Seasons Hotel George V is ideally located in the most fashionable quarter of Paris. The Arc de Triomphe, Place de la Concorde and Eiffel Tower are a short stroll away, and the grand haute couture fashion houses such as Dior, Chanel and Givenchy line the neighbouring elegant streets.

Certain hotels around the world distinguish themselves by the impact of their entrance; the George V is such a hotel. A key contribution to the initial visual effect comes from the dozens of lavish floral designs by Jeff Leatham, who creates a new theme each week using over 15,000 Dutch blooms for his fabulous innovative arrangements. The distinctive 1920s Art Deco façade opens into the chic marbled reception hall where striking towers of blossoms salute guests as they enter. Jeff believes that 'flowers bring out the passion in people, exuding energy, colour and light' – and there's nowhere better than Paris to make such a statement.

Romanesque marble statues depicting spring, summer, autumn and winter rest on pillars in the corners of the lobby, as guests come and go through the constantly revolving main doors. Ever efficient Four Seasons staff, dressed in chic tailored uniforms, swiftly welcome you with their renowned personal attention to detail, before whisking you up to your room. They live up to the high standards of service that Four Seasons has banked its reputation on – and outrank every other hotel in Paris for courtesy and care. After the hotel's reopening in 1999, General Manager Didier Le Calvez must be delighted with the results he has achieved while overseeing its meticulously planned rebirth. Its success is a tribute to his integrity and scrupulous attention to detail.

All 245 bedrooms and suites are decorated in a delicate palette of creams and beige with classical French furnishings, creating an ambience of elegance and supreme comfort. With the most spacious guest rooms in Paris, even the smallest 'superior rooms' are surprisingly large, and include a king-sized bed, large fitted closet, various objets d'art and Art Deco details. Bathrooms reflect the colour scheme of the bedrooms with either blue or green marble trimming, and there are

Entrance Hall. (opposite) **Jeff Leatham floral display.**

additional luxuries of thick terry bathrobes and an abundance of fragrant Bulgari toiletries and white orchids. Thirty of the bedrooms and suites have private balconies and terraces overlooking the city's rooftops and the night-lit Eiffel Tower, which sparkles effervescently like a champagne firework.

The hotel's four dining venues offer a variety of cuisine and style. While breakfast is best taken in your room or in the stylish La Galerie lobby restaurant, the airy Marble Courtyard is refreshingly cool during the summer months and ideally located for a light lunch. Four Seasons has every right to be proud of Le Cinq, its three Michelin-starred restaurant under the executive chef Philippe Legendre. From the start, Legendre was given carte blanche to express his culinary

creativity, selecting only the finest products that convey a variety of definitive regional tastes from across France. The sauces are his main signature and, while never over-whelming the dish, they underline the vividness of the flavours.

The restaurant's staggering success is a tribute to Legendre's mastery – it took a mere two months to achieve the first star, quite a feat bearing in mind that successful entrants must pass a minimum of five blind tests in order to be rated. The savoury tart of artichokes and Périgord black truffle, smoked Brittany lobster with morel mushrooms, and raspberry croquant garnished with hibiscus flowers are just a sample of the unforgettable combinations special to Le Cinq. Dining here is pure theatre, with all the incumbent props,

drama and attention. Beehive mounds of St Malo butter are presented under miniature glass cloches, while small side tables are reverently placed next to your chair for your handbag, or, as is frequently la mode in France, your *petit chien* in handbag.

The cellars, housing over 40,000 bottles, are a testament to sommelier Eric Beaumard's passion for authenticity and represent the world's greatest vineyards, including over a hundred different champagne varieties, an 1834 Madeira and 1947 Petrus (still available for a mere 8,500 Euros).

In the basement, the newly renovated Louis XVI-styled spa and health club are decorated in colourful trompe l'oeil murals of the gardens of Versailles. It's well equipped with a decent-sized swimming pool and

(opposite) **Le Cinq restaurant.**   **Louis XVI Spa.**   **Deluxe Suite.**

Jacuzzi, a gymnasium, saunas, steam baths, eleven treatment rooms and a hair salon. A special shiatsu room has been created according to Japanese traditions, and a lengthy menu of bespoke facial and massage treatments defines this spa as one of the city's top pamper zones. Do try the new Moroccan argon oil treatment; it leaves your skin feeling as soft as silk.

Paris is a city full of attractions and views. You can climb the Eiffel Tower, the Arc de Triomphe, the south tower of the Notre Dame or the dome of the Sacré Coeur and choose your favourite panorama. You could take a whole year off just to wander the mile upon mile of art galleries and museums. All the major European schools of art are represented, and the Louvre is home to the most recognised face in the world, the Mona Lisa with her enigmatic smile. The list of masterpieces is endless: the purest work of Van Dyck, Brueghel, Vermeer, Holbein, Rembrandt,

Reynolds, Constable, Turner, Goya, Picasso, Degas, Gauguin and Delacroix – and many more.

One of the charms of Paris is that the external aesthetics of the buildings are just as awe-inspiring as the art held within – so much so that it wasn't until my ninth visit that I actually stepped inside the Louvre. Streets have a cafe-life charm specific to the city, celebrated in art throughout the centuries. It's a simple joy just to amble along the boulevards, pausing every so often for a *café au lait* and to absorb the setting and watch the world go by. Paris is emphatically one of those places you find yourself promising to revisit after every stay – and when you do return you wonder why you left it so long.

The Month

Paris enjoys a moderate climate with wet winters and little snowfall. July days are warm and pleasant with low humidity and long

sunny days – perfect for people-watching in cafes and terraces. Each year on 14 July festivities and fireworks commemorate the storming of the Bastille in 1789 – celebrations are particularly colourful in Paris, where thousands of spectators flock to watch the ceremonies. July is the perfect month to enjoy the city's street life, before locals make the mass exodus to the south in August, leaving the city somewhat deserted.

La Bastide de Marie

France

Located in the heart of the Luberon region of southern France, the sleepy town of Ménerbes is one of Provence's most picturesque villages – half-way between the hilltop town of Gordes and rustic Bonnieux, perched on the hillside overlooking the surrounding vines, olives and cherry groves. In the afternoon the clear Provençal light, so loved by Cézanne for its purity of shades and colours, casts long shadows across the fields towards the limestone scree of Mont Ventoux that dominates the views on the eastern horizon. The melodies of birds (so rarely heard in France) carry across the air, along with the heady smells of local produce being prepared in farmhouse kitchens.

A stone's throw from the village lies La Bastide de Marie, a rambling eighteenth-century Provençal farmhouse built from rough-cut milky-coloured stone with a typical terracotta canal-tiled roof. Surrounded by twenty-four hectares of vines, the various lawns are interspersed with lavender walks, rows of cypress trees, magnolias, eucalyptus and a spectacular tilleul tree. The terrace around the property is separated from the vines by a low wall decorated with pots brimming with geraniums, roses, lavender, rosemary and succulents. Each line of well-cultivated vines ends with a solitary white rose, but it is not just ornamental – vintners across the world customarily plant roses next to vines as their wilting signals the first sign of botrytis.

From the grounds, several doors lead into the main house. Spreading across various levels, the drawing room forms the nucleus for activity, with sofas positioned around a huge stone fireplace. The subtle fragrances of Provence are reflected in the decor's muted shades of blue, purple, sage and grey, and opposite the fireplace a thick stone wall has been converted to form an immense book-shelf, chock-a-block with antique volumes. Caned chaise longues with old-fashioned boaters sitting on them face the picture window with its charming view.

Each of the twelve bedrooms, including four suites, is aptly named after a local plant: rose, green anis, mauve aster, grey sage, yellow mimosa, vanilla... and is appropriately furnished in corresponding tones. Bedroom decor reflects the simple paysanne setting, with brick floors and uneven plastered walls washed in pastel shades, adorned with distinctive Picasso pen and ink images framed in heavy wooden frames or floral oil paintings. Many rooms have a regional wrought-iron four-poster dressed in beige linen drapes, and most have a small wooden bureau, a comfortable armchair, and an antique linen press acting as a wardrobe. Bathrooms echo chic-minimalism with bare stone walls and floors, large mirrors, limestone bath surrounds and a basket of locally produced lavender and olive based toiletries.

Following their huge success with La Ferme de Marie in Mégève, owners Jocelyne and Jean-Louis Sibuet found themselves charmed in an instant by the subtleness of La Bastide and decided to create a home away from home. Jean-Louis had an added incentive;

(opposite) **Provençal chic.** **Lunch in the shade.** **Tiered swimming pool.**

he succumbed to his passion for wine, and has created his own winery. The spotless cellar has been decorated with various works of art, and is dominated by two large sculptured lamps made up from hundreds of clear glass bulbs to resemble a giant bunch of grapes. Wine lovers will savour the marriage of Grenache and Cinsault, resulting in a superlative fruity rosé, closely matched by the generous red and the honeyed apricot tones of the white.

Wherever you are on the estate, you can smell the soothing aroma of lavender blossom and the comforting wafts of home cooking from the open-fronted kitchen. Each day starts with breakfast on the east terrace, in front of the powder-blue arched barn doors, overlooking the vineyard and designer fitted kitchen. Unlike most hotels, where the kitchen is hidden from prying eyes, here gastronomy is the celebrated heart of the establishment and the importance of food

reigns supreme. A mouth-watering feast of flaky croissants, hot from the oven, served with local preserves, sweet-smelling melons and freshly ground coffee, is the perfect way to start the day.

Lunch is best taken by the pool or under one of the trees on the south terrace with a glass of the domain's chilled rosé. As an alternative, you would do well to try La Bastide (no connection) in the picturesque village of nearby Gordes. The restaurant spills down in terraces, with long views across the valley and delicious fare to match the vista.

Each night, apéritifs are served on the terrace at 7.30 p.m. accompanied by local tapas of saucisson, olives, tapenades, and freshly baked almonds that squeak on your teeth when you bite them. Dinner is a theatrical affair and each course is served on an unusual array of ceramic and glass plates. Surrounded by aromatic plants, the chef uses various herbs by the handful in his regional dishes.

House specialities include a caviar of aubergine with chorizo and crispy zucchini florets, baby pork garnished with a dramatic flaming pine cone, followed by freshly picked nectarines baked in vine leaves, with almond ice-cream on a frangipani base.

Days are long and hot, and the intense midday heat often calls for a dip in one of the two swimming pools. The smaller of the two wraps around the main building with a suntrap terrace, while the other has been transformed from a fish pond into a double-tiered rectangular pool linked by a cascade of water, surrounded by lush green lawns.

In this area of outstanding natural beauty, there's plenty to explore – you could even have a bird's-eye view of the region from a hot-air balloon. Market lovers have the choice of a different local market for every day of the week, while for the sporty there's golf in L'Isle sur Sorgue and tennis in Apt. Bicycles are readily available, and numerous walking

Dining room. **Light and shade on the east terrace.** (opposite) **Individual bedrooms.**

trails lead directly from the property. Nearby attractions include the thirteenth-century Chateau Ansouis, the fabulous lavender fields that surround the monastery at Sénanque, the unmissable Palais du Pape in Avignon and nearby Pont du Gard. Appropriately, Ménerbes has a corkscrew museum, and there's a lavender museum in nearby Coustellet.

At La Bastide de Marie, harmony has been achieved between the landscape, oenology and gastronomy in a uniquely relaxed yet elegant manner. As you wander past the local estate agent, don't be surprised if you find yourself dreaming of what it would be like to spend a year in Provence.

The Month

July's long sunny days see the drifts of lavender surrounding the property in full bloom, fragrant wafts spreading into the air as walkers brush past the flowers. The grapes on the vines are starting to swell and the groves of cherry trees are laden with their harvest of ruby marbles. Music festivals regularly take place this month in nearby Ménerbes and Cavaillon, as well as the *fêtes du miel, du melon, du pain* and *des produits régionaux*. July also sees Avignon celebrate its summer festival. It remains light each night until almost ten o'clock, when the sun sets behind the cypress trees of La Bastide, turning the sky into a stripy tie-dye of pastel blues and pinks.

The Okavango Delta

Orient-Express Safari Camps

Botswana

The increasing demand for compelling new experiences that remove western travellers from their familiar world has meant that safari has never been more in vogue. While much of Africa's plains have gained a reputation for dozens of jeeps swarming around small prides of lions, Botswana's standing has remained comparatively unblemished. As a late developer on the tourism front, Botswana appears to have learnt some lessons from her sister countries and is sensitively developing low-impact eco-friendly tourism where man and nature can enjoy a complementary role, balancing preservation and recreation.

Botswana's diverse terrain includes desert, swamp, flat pans, hardveld, quartz hills and of course the stupendous Okavango Delta in the Kalahari Desert, which covers eighty-four per cent of the country and remains one of the world's last great wilderness areas.

Each year it is not Botswana's rainfall that floods the plains, but the torrent that spills out from neighbouring Angola. After five months of bottle-necking around the Panhandle the

welcome floods create a thriving, lush ecological paradise in the Delta that attracts an annual pilgrimage of animals and bird life. They come in their droves.

Orient-Express has chosen this remote corner of Africa for its fly-in safari camps – located deep in the unspoilt northern reaches of Botswana close to the neighbouring borders of Namibia and Zimbabwe. Three stirringly romantic camps have been built in three unique eco-systems: flooded alluvial waterways around the Panhandle; broad leaved woodland with arid seasonal swamps; and dry savanna grasslands.

As a company, Orient-Express is passionately committed to providing an experience that, while luxurious, is still environmentally friendly. To ensure minimal impact on their surroundings, all camps are sensitively managed – this area of Botswana is a place of peace and perfection with a bountiful heritage, and they want to keep it that way.

Guests can choose to stay in the camps in any order or for any length of time, according

to their preferences. Eagle Island nestles near the heart of the classic fan-shaped Delta on the main southerly channel of the flood plains; Khwai River Lodge is situated in the Khwai community area bordering Moremi Game Reserve in the north-east extremity of the Delta; and Savute Elephant Camp lies on the dry cracked earth of the Savute Channel within the Chobe National Park.

For all these destinations, international travellers are met at Maun airport and flown to the camp's private airstrip by light aircraft – the only feasible way to access each area. Flying over the vast Delta plains in a small Cessna bush plane is like swallowing an *Out of Africa* pill and being instantly transported into the movie roles played by Meryl Streep and Robert Redford. There is also a practical advantage to arriving by plane: it is much easier to appreciate the differing eco-systems from the aerial viewpoint and thereby orientate yourself.

On touching down, a group of staff members congregate to sing their rapturous

Tented luxury at Savute.

welcome, placing a wreath of water lilies round your neck before leading you to your room. The twelve to fourteen tented structures in each camp are really luxurious thatched hideaways with canvas walls and ensuite facilities. Each tent is based on sturdy stilts, to protect from over-curious hippos as well as flooding. They have a spacious viewing deck, ideal as an outdoor sitting room, with opportunities to view game from the comfortable canvas hammock. At dawn you can stand on your private balcony, a silent witness to nature's masterpiece, marvelling as a family of giraffes wander peacefully across the horizon.

Interiors are decorated in suitably mannish tones without sacrificing comfort. There's a welcome absence of external telephone access, radio or CD player, leaving nature's music to entertain your senses. Safety is paramount – there's an intercom for twenty-four-hour contact with camp managers – and your comfort is guaranteed with the only air-conditioned tents in the Delta.

Around the three camps, pathways are illuminated after dusk with decorative lanterns, and at turndown a scroll telling an ancient bedtime tale from the African bush such as 'The Squirrel's Guilt-stained Coat' is placed on your pillow. As the tiny bell frogs begin a nocturnal concert, a parade of curious sounds guarantees a few nervous gasps. Rest assured – the deep roaring grunts reverberating

like laughter are only a pod of hippos mowing the grass, and the rasping cough like a saw cutting wood is just a leopard calling to its mate. You'll soon get used to it.

At each camp guests can enjoy a refreshing dip in the swimming pool, or indulge in the well-stocked reference library full of safari books and wildlife videos.

Botswana is one the world's most sparsely populated countries, the size of France but supporting a population of only one and a half million – the peace-loving Tswana people. They measure wealth in terms of cattle and name their currency the pula which, appropriately for this colossal parched land, means rain. A management couple hosts each camp, but for most of the staff this has always been home. An environmentalist and local guides *au fait* with all the vagaries of the wild – boasting instant recognition of over a hundred bird calls – accompany game-drives. At six foot five, Onx, the regional environmentalist and camp manager at Savute, certainly makes you feel safe. His love of the bush and its people combined with his desire to delight guests is very evident, while the contagious passion for the Delta from Mighty (a guide at Eagle Island) ensures a generous sharing of knowledge during any excursion.

Available activities are totally dependent upon the water levels, but generally each morning starts at 5.30 for the first game-drive. All around animals are taking advantage of

the cool dawn temperatures to hunt. The unseasoned safari-goer will be hoping to spot the 'Big Five' of lion, leopard, buffalo, elephant and rhino, which are all plentiful and regularly spotted. Equally fascinating but less conspicuous are the 'Small Five', including ant-lion, elephant shrew, rhino beetle, leopard tortoise and red-billed buffalo weaver. Bird lovers hanker after their own version of the 'Big Five': the martial eagle, southern ground hornbill, Pel's fishing owl, saddle-billed stork and kori bustard.

Thankfully, guests staying in the camp find their food far more easily than the surrounding animals. Meal times revolve around game-drives. Each repast is an amazing feat of planning and execution, starting each day with a hearty brunch served after the morning game-drive at 11 o'clock. Afternoon game-drives often coincide with tea or sundowners, as you return to camp for an aperitif served in a semi-circle around a glowing camp fire. Three-course dinners are the main social gathering of the day, when guests exchange their tales of the day's tracking.

Following dinner, gazing at the bejewelled African sky through one of the brand-new Meade DS114 telescopes is a popular pastime, especially with an indigenous digestif of Amarula liqueur in hand.

Botswana represents what remains of the old Africa. It undoubtedly has a harsh land-scape, but is brimming with abundant

(opposite) **Eagle Island Camp.**

breathtaking expanses of untamed beauty. Experience it now while it exists.

Eagle Island Camp

Eagle Island is perched on the rim of the untarnished Xaxaba (island of tall trees) Lagoon that leads off the Boro Channel in the south-western Delta wetlands of the Moremi Wildlife Reserve. The lofty indigenous trees provide welcome shade from the blistering African sun as you scrutinise the myriad waterways that meander through the vast flood-plains. These plains are home to a prolific diversity of bird and animal wildlife. This ecological wonderland attracts eighty-five per cent of Botswana's bird species and it's home to the highest concentration of fish eagles on earth – making the area an ornithologist's paradise. Built to be camouflaged as part of its surroundings, the camp affords the chance for a close encounter with any number of creatures.

The Fish Eagle Bar set out on a small promontory has been voted the world's most romantic bar, and is the ideal location to savour the spectacular African sunset with its mesmerising kaleidoscope of burnished hues

and treasure chest of wildlife.

The most obvious thrill at Eagle Camp is a ride in a *mokoro*, a dugout canoe and the local people's traditional form of transport. It's a tranquil experience, gliding along as the silent dip of the pole propels the boat through the labyrinth of clear channels, lagoons and swamps, brushing mutely against the reeds and sun-kissed water lilies. As a malachite kingfisher with its stunning plumage darts from reed to reed in search of an occasional fish splashing to the surface, you soon become oblivious to time as you daydream in the peacefulness.

The *mokoro* and island walking trail safari offers an intimate picture of the sensitively balanced circle of life and a sensuous taste of the Okavango.

Khwai River Lodge

One of the oldest and most established of all Botswana's lodges is the Khwai River Lodge, perched on the northern periphery of the Moremi Wildlife Reserve. Shaded by ancient leadwood and fig trees and with a panoramic view overlooking the Khwai

River flood plains next to the reserve, this is a natural hideout where you can cool off in the deliciously icy waters of the pool only metres away from grazing hippos and elephants.

The Khwai River marks the easternmost tip of the great alluvial fan and the northern boundary of the Moremi Reserve. It's called the predators' realm – and with good reason: vast herds of antelope pass through the game reserve each year, tracked by hungry big cats. When you see those cats lounging torpidly in the midday sun, it's hard to believe that they're such lethal killers. Sightings of lions around Khwai River have never been better, with more local kills than ever recorded. There are also excellent sightings of elephant, hippo, leopard, giraffe and hyena. And all around, exquisite expansive vistas make it so easy to understand why unspoilt Botswana is a land truly respected by its people.

Khwai River Lodge has another attraction. The Naturally Wild Spa offers a chance to indulge in a masterfully soothing massage on your own private deck using a special blend of oils, sourced exclusively from natural African

Khwai River Lodge.

plants. These include plants like macadamia, marula, geranium and black pepper.

Savute Elephant Camp

Savute Elephant Camp is set in the heart of the arid Chobe National Park, where the rugged scenery strikes a sharp contrast to the other two camps. The harsh craggy terrain makes for an even stronger sensation of wilderness and abandonment. The erratic Savute Channel, which last saw water twenty-two years ago, opens into the Savute Marsh, a vast area of a hundred square kilometres, once a perennial wetland but for now a semi-desert. Botswana's unusual geology has given this river the phenomenal ability to switch itself on and off every few decades, and for now, as the camp's name suggests, it has one of the largest elephant populations in Africa.

This bone-dry desert with 'bushveld' vegetation made up of low-lying shrubs and trees is a surprising home to these hungry pachyderms. It's a privilege to observe herds

of elephants as well as leopards, while huge prides of lion come to quench their thirst in the pumped water hole directly in front of the lodge. The silky ear-shaped pods of the towering *Acacia erioloba* trees are the elephants' favourite treat – they regularly stretch their trunks past the camp's fence to indulge their insatiable appetites.

Normally the elephant, as the largest land creature on earth, reigns supreme, but recently a large pride of Savute lions has bizarrely taken to stalking elephants – a phenomenon not encountered anywhere else in the world. Giant abandoned carcasses are only too obvious proof of their success.

Before you leave, make sure you dine bush-style in the traditional *boma* – a meeting place used by senior tribesmen for *kgotlas* (meetings) – built entirely from local driftwood from around Savute. It's an atmospheric tribal experience with spectacular vistas of the African skies silhouetted by the camel thorn trees.

By exploring the Okavango with Orient-

Express, you witness nature in the raw, while never going without the comforts of home.

The Month

The winter months between June and August are considered the best for viewing game. They're characterised by pleasantly dry, cloudless days and cold nights when the temperature drops sharply to between minus 5°C and 10°C (22–50°F).

The annual ebb and flow of the Delta's flood waters starts in May, a whole six months after the springs high up on the Bengwela Plateau have dispatched them. By July they are close to reaching their peak, only to start receding in advance of the following year's rainfall.

Guests can take advantage of the high water levels at Eagle Island for rides in a *mokoro* or speedier motorboat – particularly useful, when viewing larger game, for zooming right up close and then making a hasty exit if necessary.

August

Claridge's

London

'Not that I intend to die, but when I do, I don't want to go to heaven, I want to go to Claridge's.' Many a guest would agree with the words of actor Spencer Tracy after staying in this Art Deco jewel set in the heart of Mayfair in London's West End.

As a little girl, I used to love the television series *The Duchess of Duke Street*, and stepping into Claridge's always felt like playing a small role in that period drama. The second you walk into the stylish world of London's undisputed doyen of hotels you inadvertently adopt a different stance, as if you become a player yourself. It's hardly surprising that some of the hotel's aura rubs off on you, because ever since it opened its doors it has epitomised elegant grandeur.

The hotel began its rich history in 1812 as a tiny establishment in just one building, and was known as Mivart's after the owner. It soon spilled into the five neighbouring houses along Brook Street and by 1853 (the dawn of the age of the railway hotel) a letter in

The Times newspaper claimed that there were just three first-class London hotels, of which Mivart's was one.

In 1854, when Mivart retired, William and Marianne Claridge took over the property and gave it their name. Its reputation continued to grow and grow, and in 1860 it received the ultimate seal of approval when Queen Victoria visited Empress Eugénie of France who was in residence at the hotel. A lack of funds led to the takeover of the hotel by Richard D'Oyly Carte in December 1893, on the suggestion of César Ritz. The hotel you see today is the work of C.W. Stephens, already famous for rebuilding Harrods, who was commissioned to demolish the original buildings and replace them with the distinguished seven-storey hotel.

The new Claridge's opened its doors in 1898 and since then has played host to virtually every head of state, and celebrities galore, priding itself on its policy of complete discretion. Yet it was in the Art Deco period,

back in the 1920s and 30s, when it really burst on to the London social scene.

During the Second World War Claridge's became a haven for exiled royalty, including the monarchs of Norway, Greece, Yugoslavia and The Netherlands. Winston Churchill even declared Suite 212 Yugoslavian territory for a day on 17 July 1944, when Crown Prince Alexander II was born there. In one way or another some Yugoslavian soil was found and sprinkled under the bed so the prince would be born on home ground. Indeed, the hotel became a home away from home for many a crowned head, so much so that in 1947, before the wedding of the then Princess Elizabeth, a harassed diplomat telephoned Claridge's and asked to speak to the King. 'Certainly, sir,' was the response, 'to which King do you want to speak?'

Kings and commoners alike enter the hotel through the newly restored Deco foyer, once an awkward old-fashioned carriage drive entrance, the polished black and white marble

The Fumoir. (opposite) **Gordon Ramsey's restaurant.**

floor steering you into the well-appointed reading room. In the lobby an open fire crackles constantly in front of the sweeping staircase leading to first-floor suites.

The hotel boasts 203 individually designed spacious bedrooms and suites with no two alike. Guests have a choice of styles, and can plump for exquisite Art Deco, the more traditional Victorian, or one of the six newly designed executive suites decorated in rich contemporary tones with a 42-inch plasma TV screen, a handsome writing desk and distinctively lit bar. Many rooms feature antique mantelpieces, and three 'piano suites' hold grand pianos, one of which belonged to Richard D'Oyly Carte. Every room has retained its old-fashioned call button to summon the waiter, valet or maid. Bathrooms are generally huge modified versions of marble and glass 1920s originals, overflowing with crested towels and Floris unguents.

Dining has always been an essential ingredient of the hotel's experience. Legend has it that Table 131 in the old Claridge's Restaurant was called The Royal Box because it was set discreetly inside the alcove at the side of the room, making it popular with kings, presidents and prime ministers. Another table is referred to as the Greek Cantina because Aristotle Onassis regularly chose to sit there, while the late novelist, Dame Barbara Cartland, had a permanent table reserved for her for fifty years, always covered in pink flowers.

Guests can enjoy a quintessentially English afternoon tea in the newly renovated reading room while browsing through one of the leather-bound photograph albums of renowned guests who have stayed in the hotel over the last century. Before dining, have an aperitif in the glorious Art Deco bar or in the purple fumoir – a room lined with poster-sized black and white Dietrichesque photographs of ladies smoking.

Today, celebrity chef Gordon Ramsay offers the most scrumptious dining experience in London. The stylish decor of the dining room has reinterpreted the historic space, using original plush aubergine, plum and apricot tones, custom-designed furniture and soft furnishings. Three-tiered, apricot-shaded chandeliers cast agreeable and intimate light on each table, as the team of expert unobtrusive waiters present course after course of flavourful enjoyment.

With three prestigious Michelin stars, Gordon Ramsay heads the brigade of thirty-five in his newly outfitted kitchen. Seamless service is guaranteed with the installation of CCTV above the production line of chefs' hats – back of house has never been slicker. Within the kitchen, tucked to one side of the chef's 'pass', is the most entertaining table for dining in London – Gordon's Chef's Table. Here, for £700 for a six-course dinner

Davies Penthouse Suite.

(excluding wine), you have a ringside seat to view the finest cooking in England and the full drama of a superbly run kitchen brigade for the entire evening.

Claridge's continues to enjoy the constant patronage of royalty and 'A' list celebrities more than any other London venue. It's often dubbed the 'Palace's Annexe', due to the tradition for foreign heads of state, who are guests of the British monarch at Buckingham Palace from Monday to Wednesday, to move to Claridge's on Thursday, and return the hospitality by hosting a banquet for the monarch that evening.

The good life continues on the sixth floor, where the newly created Olympus Suite has warm-up and workout rooms,

a steam room and treatment areas offering body massage, shiatsu, facial and spa treatments using Anne Sémonin and La Prairie products. Personal training sessions, weight training and aerobic facilities are easily arranged, plus use of the Berkeley's swimming pool and golf at Wentworth golf club. On the ground floor other top-notch amenities include a traditional barber, a John Frieda hair salon and the Edward Goodyear florist – who also does the exquisite hotel flower arrangements.

In the twenty-first century, Claridge's remains the epitome of luxury, style and Art Deco elegance, and is so much more than just somewhere to lay your head.

The Month

London always has something exciting in store for visitors of any age. Shoppers will love the designer boutiques of nearby Bond Street, South Molton Street and Regent Street at any time of year, but balmy August days are perfect for a visit to the zoo, picnicking in the parks, or attending an open air theatre or opera production in Holland Park. A scenic cruise down the River Thames to Hampton Court avoids traffic jams and casts a new perspective on the capital's evolving skyline. The BBC Promenade Concerts run through August at the Royal Albert Hall, and at the end of the month thousands flock to the Notting Hill Carnival.

Skibo Castle

Scotland

The Nordic name 'Skibo' has various interpretations, but no one disputes Andrew Carnegie's description of his glorious Highland castle and estate as 'heaven on earth'. Its wonder has enchanted generations for over a thousand years. Inconspicuously tucked away on the Dornoch Firth, Skibo benefits from a remarkable microclimate affording record sunshine hours and low rainfall.

It's worthwhile taking the slightly longer road to Skibo, approaching the estate from Struie Hill, the route taken by Carnegie himself before today's iron bridge existed. In August, the hour-long drive from Inverness passes crops of carrots and potatoes and fields of golden corn ripe for harvesting. Along the road, lime-green pastures are scattered with distinctive Highland cattle grazing among the bright yellow ragwort, gorse and rosebay willow herb. Red kites soar overhead along the Moray Firth, and the occasional salmon jumps in the River Alness. As you follow the Dornoch Firth from Bonar Bridge, a huge 4,000-year-old

monolith known simply as the 'standing stone' dominates the horizon.

Skibo was bought by Carnegie in 1898 to host the activities of his philanthropic and social life. Its guest-book reads like a *Who's Who* of Edwardian history: Rudyard Kipling, Lloyd George, the Rockefellers – and King Edward VII, who was so impressed with the revolutionary hot and cold running water and central heating system that he incorporated them into his renovation plans for Buckingham Palace a few years later.

In 1990 the castle was converted into a club for private members seeking refuge from a hectic world. Three years of building and £20 million later the estate was transformed into the 'private golf and sporting club' enjoyed today. Members are treated as house guests of a great 7,500-acre estate where the food, accommodation, style and service are unmatched – where else on earth is one greeted at the steps with a glass of home-bottled sloe gin? The estate falls into

two parts: the grouse moors, deer forests and lochs opening out on to the 'flow-country' of Caithness and Sutherland; and the castle with its landscaped parklands and immaculately cultivated gardens sweeping down to the Dornoch Firth.

The castle is the main hub of activity where the magnificent reception rooms have lost none of their glorious heyday charm, awash with antiques and memorabilia. As you relax in the drawing room, warming cold toes at the roaring fire while tucking into delicious Earl Grey tea and divine shortbread, the view of the rose garden offers a timeless pleasure.

You can even sit in the library, crammed with priceless vellum-bound books, and write a letter at Carnegie's diminutive desk (he was only five-foot-one). For those who have an avid passion for cigars, Skibo has its very own cigar room equipped with castle memorabilia and humidifiers.

In the castle there are twenty-one bedroom suites with huge Victorian baths and basins,

(opposite) **Old-style luxury.** **Tiled bathrooms.**

intricately tiled floors, cosy open fires and magnificent views across the estate. The original canopied four-poster beds and oriental carpets are complemented by framed photographs of today's members at play.

The secluded lodges provide added privacy and are a fantastic way for families to enjoy the estate at full volume without disturbing the peace enjoyed by other guests. Of the twelve lodges, the most unusual is definitely the Dairy – comprising the bathroom, where milk and cream were originally bottled, and the bedroom, where the final products were packed prior to distribution. In both rooms the original Delft wall tiles, marble shelves and even stained-glass windows remain unchanged, faithfully preserved in their original state. Under the carpet lies a white marble fountain, which together with the flooded shelves and unusually shaped roof would have stabilised the cool atmosphere necessary in a dairy.

No creature comfort has been forgotten in this scrumptious suite. As you enter, the redolent Scottish tones of 'Evelix' play on the CD, next to which stands a tartan tray laden with decanters of the finest gin, sherry and, of course, malt whisky. The unusual prop of a pillar-bookcase in the centre is filled with tomes of a bygone era and dominates the bathroom. It would be all too easy to retreat to this private space without setting foot outside all weekend!

In August, huge pots of seasonal mauve heather decorate the rooms, and unexpected personal possessions such as hot-water bottles and board games lie hiding in the antique coffers. At night it is impossible to resist one last malt or 'Scottish tablet' (placed in tartan jars at the bedside to starve off midnight munchies) before slipping into Peter Reed's finest linen and drifting off to sleep in the supremely comfortable bed.

Throughout the estate are vigilant but gracious 'hosts' whose staggering attention to detail and dedicated teamwork ensure an unforgettable stay. This grand castle is full of charming, if a little eccentric, characters; many have lived on the estate all their lives and see their jobs not as work but as a way of life. Something they all hold in common is an awe and respect for their surroundings and a sense of privilege to work and live in such beauty. James, the butler, once worked as a porter at a British Rail station – he's clearly found his true home at Skibo and vows never to leave (even though a little tempted by some of the numerous Hollywood offers). Alan, recognised as the castle's appointed court jester and dinner host, is a true comedian – just refrain from telling him that he resembles Billy Connolly!

Life at Skibo has changed little in the last century. Each morning at eight o'clock a bagpiper in Highland dress circles the castle to stir guests from their slumber. They then descend the main staircase to the sound of grand organ music filling the castle. While much of the original furniture has never left the castle, endeavours to track down many other pieces – including the main dining table – have paid huge dividends.

Dining is one of the great delights of Skibo. A full Scottish buffet-breakfast taken in Mrs Carnegie's dining room starts the day with a happy constitution. Lunch is best taken in the clubhouse enjoying the magnificent views across the links.

Fairytale castle. **Grand staircase.** (opposite) **Gourmet dining.**

Dinner is a unique house party affair. Cocktails are served in the main hall, from which guests follow the piper to Mr Carnegie's stately dining room where all are seated around the lavishly decorated oak table. The host, who has carefully orchestrated the seating plan (I found myself seated between an international banking god and a fascinating brain surgeon!), commences with an anecdotal tale and then rises for a toast to Carnegie. The gastronomic three-course dinners and gourmet wines are masterfully composed. The finishing touch is provided by Skibo's signature 'Scottish tablet', served with coffee, liqueurs and cigars in the main hall or members' lounge.

The choice of activities is abundant, and while you could easily spend a morning at the Clarin's spa enjoying a facial or massage or lapping the Olympic-sized pool, other delights keep you vigorous. Every morning Andrew MacLeod, Skibo's falconer, and his sixteen barn owls, falcons and eagles put on a fine display, entertaining and educating guests in this ancient and bloody sport. Among many other choices in the daily itinerary are fly fishing for speckle-bellied trout or wild salmon in the lochs with expert gillie Michael, clay-pigeon shooting, roaming the estate on one of the estate's own thoroughbreds at a healthy gallop, or haring around in a four-wheel-drive off-road.

And of course there's the golf... Skibo has not one but two courses of its own. Members describe the pretty nine-hole parkland course as 'the next best thing to your own private course'. Carnegie's original golf course has been reconstructed into an outstanding eighteen-hole championship links course with views across Struie Hill and the waters of the Firth. Within twenty minutes of the estate are nine other golf courses (known as Scotland's necklace), including the legendary Royal Dornoch. This is golfers' paradise!

The Month

August is almost always the warmest month of the year in Scotland, with the opportunity to enjoy the longest number of outdoor hours on the estate. Its northern latitude brings the midnight sun, and the peninsula itself is blessed with the lowest annual rainfall and the most days of sunshine in Scotland. Relaxed barbecues and long days of outdoor pursuits fill the month before the colours change, dominated by the mountain heathers and piercing autumn light. (Apparently midges can be a problem some years – although more so on the west coast – and we saw them only once when we were riding across a boggy meadow.)

While I prefer August, the winter months have their own special charm. Then, the estate takes on a fairytale personality, especially when blanketed in snow. Impenetrable dark cloaks the castle by teatime and the inviting shelter of roaring log fires and warm light can be seen for miles around. It is true to say that the huge choice of indoor and outdoor pursuits at Skibo can be enjoyed year-round, and relying on good summer weather anywhere in the British Isles is a gamble. Just make sure you take your warmest clothes!

Other key times to visit are Hogmanay, with the traditional three-day non-stop New Year party, or later in January for 'Burns Night', combining the finest malt, haggis and lashings of poetry. The quieter springtime months offer the chance to be 'King of the Castle' with the estate to yourself. Avid golfers flock to test their skills at the May Bank Holiday Tournament before returning with their families for the summer solstice celebrations, appropriately called 'Up All Night'. The weather plays games in late autumn when the sudden changes in temperature cause ethereal sea fogs to penetrate the estate – a hot toddy is a compensatory treat for the weather. October and November are the best months if you have come to gaze at the northern lights. Each host and each guest voice a preference for their favourite time of year – take your pick and enjoy!

Chateau Lake Louise

Canada

The Indians called it the 'Lake of Little Fishes'. Thomas Wilson, working for the Canadian Pacific Railway, was the first white man to see it in 1882 and, captivated by its magical hue, named it 'Emerald Water'. It was renamed Lake Louise in honour of Queen Victoria's fourth daughter, but, whatever its name, this astonishing body of emerald-blue water has always been a vision of natural beauty among the dramatic peaks of the Canadian Rockies.

This whole area of western Canada has become a magnet for tourists – fulfilling the nineteenth-century prophecy of Canadian Pacific Railway president William Cornelius Van Horne: 'Since we cannot export the scenery, we will have to import the tourists' – and import them they certainly have. In 1885 only a dozen people made the trek to Lake Louise, while now up to 20,000 people can visit in a day – though the area is so vast that any sign of a crowd soon dissipates into the mountain range that surrounds the lake. The area remains remote and undeveloped.

Building a hotel here has played a major role in shaping some of west Canada's history – though it's hard to believe that today's Chateau Lake Louise started life as a simple one-storey, two-bedroom chalet, the first in an eclectic series of buildings culminating in this luxurious 480-room chateau. Its style is Swiss meets Canadian – a reflection of the fact that initially, the Canadian Pacific Railway employed Swiss mountain guides to teach tourist-adventurers climbing and skiing techniques. In each of the massive halls on the ground floor, giant stuffed moose, elk and bear trophies adorn every nook and cranny. The mammoth construction is a living relic of the ostentatious grandeur born of the Canadian Pacific Railway, and walls are covered with black and white photographs of the characters who have groomed its path in history.

It's true that there are smaller, cosier places to stay in Lake Louise but, once seen, the spell-binding view of the lake and soaring starkness of the ice-carved peaks known as the Plain of Six Glaciers is the only view to wake up to.

Even more special, at dawn and dusk you'll have the stunning backdrop of the Victoria Glacier and the impossibly perfect emerald water totally to yourself.

Porters clad in jaunty lederhosen and feathered caps greet you at the steps and welcome you through to the great hall – an immense space sunlit by a chain of arched picture windows and ornate chandeliers – before escorting you to your room. I would strongly recommend staying in one of the newly renovated Fairmont Gold rooms situated on the seventh floor, where three rooms have been knocked into one. Large quilted counterpanes cover king-size beds with fluffy goose-down pillows, and all lake-side rooms enjoy the spectacular panorama of the dazzling waters of the lake and the snow-capped peaks. The private lounge has the qualities of an art gallery, displaying museum paintings of indigenous wildlife, archive photographs and rows of antique books.

Other benefits of staying on this floor include an honour bar, complimentary tea

A Fairmont Gold room.   Poppy brasserie.   (opposite) Walliser Stube.

and cocktail canapés, and freshly polished shoes (or in many cases walking boots) to start the morning. The large marble bathrooms are furnished with both a bath and a walk-in shower, two vanity basins and generous baskets of Fairmont unguents.

Guests are spoilt for choice when it comes to mealtimes, with the option of six different restaurants. Breakfast can be enjoyed in either the formal Fairview Restaurant – which specialises in coast-to-coast Canadian fare and flambé desserts at dinner – or the more casual alpine-style Poppy Brasserie. Lunch is most enjoyable as a gourmet picnic on the lake or up the mountain, and can be packed in a hamper or rucksack by staff at the Chateau Deli. This is conveniently open around the clock to prepare any sandwich combination you dream up during the night.

The taking of tea is celebrated in a number of ways in and around the chateau. In the first quarter of the last century the Canadian Pacific Railway constructed three tea houses on the peaks above the chateau, serving tea from silver and fine bone china. Even the

Prince of Wales stopped for a thirst-quenching cuppa during his 'morning exercise' in September 1919. Today the tea houses at Lake Agnes and the Plain of Six Glaciers are independently run on a rather more casual basis, but are equally as welcoming.

Tea with a glass of champagne can also be enjoyed in more traditional style overlooking the superlative view from the lofty sixteen-foot windows in the Lakeview Lounge or Lobby Bar. Delicious finger-sized asparagus and smoked salmon sandwiches are followed by a tower of berry tartlets, mocha-laced opera cake, mini eclairs and scones with imported Devonshire cream. Looking around, it seems that anything goes on the dress front here – hiking boots mix with stilettos, Gortex with silk – but all who have travelled have one thing in common: they are drawn to the dreamlike vista that is featured in magazines across the globe.

For dinner, by far the most atmospheric corner of the chateau is the Walliser Stube, a library turned dining room where books have been replaced by floor-to-ceiling wine

cabinets accessed by sliding rustic loft ladders. Wooden tables, heart-carved chairs and the most adventurous fondue and raclette choices found anywhere in Canada play up the Swiss connection. And if fondue is not to your liking, the formal Victoria Room is yet another restaurant with its massive stone fireplaces, painted beams and tempting dainty *amuse-bouches* and creamy sorbets.

While the spa is still in the planning stage, guests can take advantage of the menu of in-room massages on offer or enjoy a little muscle relief from the steam room and sauna adjacent to the pool. For now, 'the gym in our great outdoors' is the name of the game – as indeed it always has been, ever since those Swiss mountain guides were brought in, establishing a healthy alpine culture. The early tourists also came to visit Lake Louise for riding, fishing and bird watching, and to sketch and paint. Today you can enjoy mountain-biking, or take a photography class or cooking course at the chateau in one of the themed activity weeks. During the brief summer months, canoeing trips depart from

(opposite) **Dinner with a view.**   **Still waters.**

a rustic log cabin on the lakeshore, while hikers can choose many of the mountain paths including the walk to Lake Agnes, also known as the 'Lake in the Clouds'. This is a smaller version of Lake Louise just above the first tea house and is surrounded by chipmunks and red squirrels.

Wannabe cowboys and cowgals can saddle up for day-long mountain trail rides at the on-site corral to trek the paths that have been followed for over a hundred years. Well-groomed horses named 'T-Bone' or 'Warrior' confidently saunter along the tracks and seem to enjoy the philosophical wisdom of gaucho guide Charles as much as the guests do.

The entire mountain experience is encapsulated in the chateau's very own home-grown naturalist and guide, Bruce Bembridge, and its extensive mountain heritage programme. This encompasses a variety of seasonal activities including hiking, snow-shoeing, stargazing, cross-country skiing and building something called a quincy – a type of

snow-hut. Bruce's knowledge of animal tracking and wild flowers is legendary, and whether you've come to huff and puff your way to the summit or just want a stroll along the lake, a morning with Bruce will leave you with a better understanding of and enhanced love for the natural world.

The Month

Chateau Lake Louise is a worthy candidate for the winter months when snow blankets the mountains and transforms the lake into a white wonderland, especially if you enjoy skiing, skating or dog sledding. However, it has long been celebrated as a premier summer resort for good reason, and to see it at its best you need to go at the height of the brief three-month summer period. Only in August when the snows have fully melted do the 'spring' flowers bloom into colour. Every native will tell you that the long August days are best for the endless recreational activities available, including meadow and mountain

picnics, hiking, canoeing, white water rafting, riding, mountain-biking and river, fly or heli-fishing.

A natural wonder trip to the Continental Divide, the point where all waters flow to either the Pacific or Atlantic Ocean, is a perfect summer excursion, as are the guided trips around the area. The water is at its deepest turquoise and the delicate spangles of red and yellow poppies strike a breathtaking contrast against the gleaming Victoria Glacier.

September

Palazzo Vendramin

at the Cipriani

Venice

As a young girl, I once turned a corner and stepped into the Piazza San Marco unprepared for what was there. The impact of what I saw will stay with me forever. It was 'Vivaldi Week' and two huge speakers, attached to the Byzantine basilica and bell tower, were throwing out the wondrous 'Four Seasons' while young ballerinas dressed in pastel chiffon floated across the square. Man had created something as beautiful as nature, and the contagious energy in the air and the utter enchantment of the scene left an indelible mark. The wonder that strikes you when visiting this city for the first, second or umpteenth time never fails to inspire your innermost self. Its beauty speaks a language that men and women of any race and nationality are able to grasp immediately.

Venice is filled with a unique mixture of sounds: bells ringing out from the dozens of church towers, water splashing at the sides of the canals as gondolas and water taxis pass, violinists practising from third-floor windows,

and men walking along the small canal alleyways suddenly breaking into song.

The timeless Rialto is a living 'Diagon Alley', lined with narrow shops selling leather-bound books, herbs, traditional masks, scented candles, soaps, Murano glass and Burano lace, ornately decorated paper and hundreds of other delights, alongside Italy's favourite fashion houses.

Across the Guidecca Canal lies one of my favourite hotels in the world. When they first opened the doors of the Cipriani in 1958, the restaurateur extraordinaire, Commendator Giuseppe Cipriani, and the enthusiastic Guinness sisters realised their dream come true: peace and privacy in Venice. The Palazzo Vendramin, a fifteenth-century residence sold to the Cipriani by the Duchess of Manchester while retaining a number of rooms for herself, is connected to the Cipriani through the beautiful Casanova Gardens via a rose loggia. Situated on the Guidecca Island on the lagoon side of Venice, it is only five minutes from the Piazza San Marco by the hotel's private

launch. With its lush gardens, it is best described as an oasis in the heart of Venice, boasting the only swimming pool and tennis court in the city.

Here, the seven butler-serviced suites are the perfect escape from the brouhaha beyond. Three of them benefit from the most spectacular views in Venice, across the Laguna towards Santa Maria della Salute and the Piazza San Marco – this has to be it for anyone searching for the ultimate 'room with a view'.

Vendramin rooms are individually decorated with priceless Murano glass appliques and chandeliers, irreplaceable antiques, ornate bureaux, Fortuny and Rubelli fabrics and hand-painted furnishings. The pastel walls are uncrowded, so as not to distract from the exquisite setting or clutter the space, and the two televisions hidden discreetly under display tables cleverly appear by remote control. Each suite has a small kitchenette and bar, giving a home-from-home atmosphere especially for longer-staying guests – making it easy and enjoyable to prepare a quick lunch

Dining alfresco at Cip's.   (opposite) **A palazzo suite.**

of fresh pasta, asparagus, basil and mozzarella brought straight from the Rialto market.

Beds are dressed in smooth Rivolta Carmignani linen sheets, while the bathrooms are filled with copious amounts of Helleboro unguents liberally scattered over the Verona red marble. A huge shower room, Jacuzzi bath and a third television hidden behind a mirror all contribute to the utter sumptuousness of the suite.

Italians are a proud people and never more so than at the Cipriani. The dignified managing director, Dr Natale Rusconi, has been 'proud to serve' since 1977. At seventy-six, he is a born hotelier, seasoned linguist, Latin scholar, gastronome, and godfather to the nurture of Venice. His culinary excellence, combined with the flair of Chef de Cuisine Renato Piccolotto, has developed the success of many house specialities such as the delicious bittersweet chocolate ice-cream or mouth-watering 'Carpaccio', specially created for a contessa on a diet. Most recently he has

recultivated the old Casanovian vineyard to create a new *vin salso* harvested by hotel staff and aged in oak casks.

The suave young Resident Manager, Patrick Nayrolles, hot from Carcassonne, is the Cipriani's new protégé, well qualified and well chosen for the role. A more venerable member of staff is Virgilio Mancin, doorman since 1958. While you wait for your launch at the jetty, take your time and spend a moment with him. His smiling face and gravelly voice are full of wisdom and helpful tips for your day's excursion. Special to the Palazzo Vendramin Suite is Guiseppe, a butler of the old school, who has looked after everyone who's ever stayed here. Either he's cloned himself or he works 24 hours a day – seemingly ever present for your every whim.

Every member of the dedicated staff makes every day special. Each morning the arousing aroma of coffee is mixed with the smell of jasmine blooms, old-fashioned scented roses and freshly cut grass wafting through the

huge window overlooking the gardens. Each day afternoon tea is served at five o'clock, and cocktails from six o'clock in the palazzo's private salon, in addition to all the dining facilities of the Cipriani.

Meals are generally served al fresco in one of the three terraces around the hotel. The newest and most contemporary restaurant is Cip's, located on the ground floor of the Palazzetto Nani Barbaro, adjacent to the Palazzo, with an outdoor terraced pontoon that has a panoramic view overlooking the Grand Canal – a restaurant, pizzeria, grill and Dolcibar – the perfect place to sip the best Bellini in town and watch the sunset as the reflections in the Laguna fade. The sublime menus in each of the four restaurants celebrate strong Italian roots. Renato Piccolotto insists on fresh market produce each day, maintaining that in the art of good cuisine there is no need to disguise the naturally robust flavours of good food.

To work off some of that good food, try the

(opposite) **Casanova Gardens.**   The private launch returns from the mainland.

huge salt-water swimming pool. If you can tear yourself away from that, the hotel also has a red clay tennis court set in the rear of the gardens, a small gym, Turkish bath, sauna, massage and hydro system.

Uncontested as Europe's most romantic city, the genius of the architecture hosts some of the world's greatest treasures. There's just so much of Venice to see – the Doge's Palace and San Marco, the Academia, the Peggy Guggenheim Collection, San Salute, San Maria dei Frari, San Giorgio Maggiore, the Rialto... and never enough time in just one trip. The streets and canals are best enjoyed at a meandering pace, wandering in and out of the dozens of churches, museums, galleries, shops, bars and restaurants. Guide books aplenty will point out the renowned, but you'll have more fun and get a greater taste of the city if you allow yourself to get lost in the maze of back streets and canals, knowing that you're never far from a square where someone can point you back in the right direction.

A day trip to the islands of Murano, Burano and Torcello is a relaxing way to escape the hubbub and enjoy another aspect of the city's famous reputation. Although you can't walk down a street without glancing at a window of Venetian glass, it's best to visit the island of Murano where most of the glass is made. The island's history dates back to 1291 when all the glassmakers' furnaces were moved there in an attempt to eliminate medieval espionage. The skills and secrets have been passed down from father to son throughout the centuries and, amazingly, many of the families of master craftsmen trading during the Renaissance continue today. Take a trip to the factory of Signoretti, where unprotected hands roll molten glass on rods at 900°C.

From Murano, it's a short boat ride to the island of Burano, where the dying art of lace making will exist for maybe only another decade. The skill takes years to master, and then each lacemaker specialises in just one of seven different intricate stitches. Twenty years ago, you would have encountered a black-clad widow in every doorway, sitting with her white cotton string. Today, they are far less ubiquitous, and the shops now supplement their sales with imported machine-made goods. Film stars are now buying up the brightly painted residences, taking the place of the artisans of previous centuries.

The atmospheric restaurant 'Da Romano' on Burano, where pictures of Venice cover every square inch of the walls, has remained unchanged and is the perfect stop for a bowl of the house special, 'Risotto Romano', served plain or with shrimp or cuttlefish – delicious. From here you can see the island of Torcello and finish the day with a visit to the church of Santa Fosca and the cathedral of Santa Maria Assunta with its magnificent mosaics.

Whatever activities your busy day involves, the retreat of the Palazzo Vendramin at the Cipriani is truly heaven on earth.

The Month
These days Venice is busy all year round, and June, July and August are heaving with day-trip tourists from cruise ships the size of towns. Apart from the famous masked carnival in February, the winter months are calmer. The best time to visit, however, is in September, when the intense summer heat has abated and the clear autumn light transforms the water and brick into a kaleidoscope of Turneresque tones. The historic regatta held on the first Sunday in September, when vessels of all sizes parade along the Grand Canal carrying passengers dressed in ancient costumes, is a true Venetian affair – and an event not to be missed.

Oberoi

Lombok

Slightly smaller than its sister island of Bali, Lombok – Indonesian for 'chilli' probably because of the ubiquitous chilli farms that cover the island – has become the new frontier of luxury travel in Indonesia. Its shores are peaceful now, but haven't always been so. The original inhabitants are thought to have hailed from north-west India and Burma, but in the early eighteenth century the neighbouring king of Sumbawa attacked Lombok. The island's celebrated Chief Datu Selaparang requested the aid of nearby Bali to repel the rival forces and, in return for their help, the Balinese were allowed to settle in Lombok. Hence the strong Balinese influence on the island, which today has a population of two-and-a-half million Muslim Sasak people.

Arriving at Lombok's Oberoi Hotel at dusk is unlike anything you'll ever experience in the echelons of world-class hotels. You begin to be aware that this tiny island holds something unusual on the busy aeroplane transfer from Singapore – the sound of excited cheers and screams from locals anticipating their

return home. A rather primitive landing at the small airport is followed by an hour's journey over pot-hole-studded roads curving their way through rocky coastal vistas and shanty villages displaying their wares of intricately carved mahogany furniture. The curious sight of various pieces of furniture alongside multi-coloured glass bottles of petrol offered for sale on every porch leaves you wondering what could possibly lie at the end of the road.

Suddenly the road bends and a driveway (illuminated at night by candlelit lanterns) leads you past lush cultivated lawns and bougainvillaea that envelop you in a sanctuary of calm and serenity. The welcome is immediate at the stunning open-air lobby, where your gaze is irresistibly drawn to one of Indonesia's largest and most picturesque swimming pools, studded with palm trees and sunken cushioned bales.

This tranquil garden resort on Lombok's idyllic Medana Beach enjoys breathtaking, far-reaching views of Bali's Mount Ajung twenty-six miles away. Set in twenty-four

acres of private grounds, the hotel's indulgent use of space and luxurious accommodation has set the standard for the Oberoi Group's new brand of hotels.

Accommodation is split between two wings of spacious luxury pavilions, and twenty stunning single-storeyed thatched-roofed villas. Rooms are air-conditioned, decorated with plush textiles and finely carved interiors, each with a four-poster bed draped in muslin mosquito nets for an authentic Lombok experience. The heavy wooden doors slide open to reveal panoramic views of the western horizon.

Marble bathrooms are set in private walled gardens with double vanities and deep baths backing on to ponds filled with plants and ginger-coloured goldfish. Luxury walk-in wardrobes and abundant Crabtree and Evelyn products are thoughtfully provided.

Dining here is a delight – and all in the open air. For breakfast or a light barefooted lunch, the informal Sunbird Cafe next to the beach and swimming pool is perfect. For dinner,

(opposite) **The Lumbung restaurant.** **Luxurious yet traditional bedrooms.** **The spa suite.**

the Lumbung restaurant offers a fine selection of Asian and Continental cuisine. There are also casual buffet dinners when you are entertained by music and dance performed in the amphitheatre. Sunset cocktails are an absolute must at either the cosy Tokek Bar overlooking the beach or on your private dais in your garden courtyard.

The Oberoi Spa offers a variety of body-pampering treatments, including traditional Indian Ayurvedic massages that concentrate on toning the body and detoxifying the internal body systems; aromatic massages producing a warming effect, improving blood circulation and relieving muscle aches; and Hawaiian massages eroding fatigue, calming the mind and restoring vital energy. Other treatments include body cleansers, body wraps and

bespoke facials and body treatments. Also included in the spa area are a gymnasium, beauty salon, and private pavilions offering sauna and herbal baths.

Lombok people are good-humoured and welcoming. None more so than 'Banana', the caring and conscientious head barman who is a star in his own right. Ask him to tell you the story of how he came to work at 'the best hotel in Lombok' while he mixes your favourite cocktail – you won't be disappointed, either by the drink or the tale.

Although it's still a relatively untouched and sleepy bolt-hole, there's plenty of adventure on the island and its surroundings. Sight-seeing in Lombok gives you a chance to see and experience a more simple way of life on an island where things have remained the same

for hundreds of years. Most of Lombok has remained virtually unexplored by tourists and untouched by the swift development of Asia. In Lombok laid-back 'rubber-time' still dominates the lifestyle and things tend to evolve at their own pace.

The multitude of attractions off the beaten track include the nearby Gili Islands, famous

Thatched villa. (opposite) **View to Bali's Mount Ajung.**

for their white sandy beaches, crystal-clear waters and fringing coral reefs affording a perfect opportunity for a short escape or a day outing. The pace of life is unhurried with the only means of transport being the *cidomo*, a local pony and cart. You don't need to take much more than snorkelling equipment, a good book, your swimsuit and a sarong – the chef will even prepare a special picnic basket lunch.

For something more adventurous, Mount Rinjani is said to be the home of the goddess Anjani, representing a spiritual and sacred link to the Sasak people of Lombok as well as the Balinese. The myth says that Rinjani was created when monkeys, playing with the moon, broke three pieces off and dropped them to earth. One piece became Mount Merapi in Java, one became Bali's Mount Angung and one Rinjani. As you climb higher

towards the cloud-piercing peak, the trail opens to spectacular vistas of the ocean and surrounding countryside. At 2,900 metres, the views are dizzying.

The largest waterfall in Lombok is worth a trek. Sedangile plunges approximately twenty metres into the natural pool below. The source of the water is the Crater Lake, Segara Anak, high above in Lombok's Rinjani volcano. You can swim in the invigoratingly cold water while your guide sets up a picnic lunch – then head back to the Oberoi for sunset at the Tokek.

For an insight into local culture, visit Masbagik Village, one of Lombok's traditional earthenware centres where the secret of the primitive production has been handed down from generation to generation. The potters produce an incredible variety of subtly coloured traditional ware, used for many purposes,

including the preparation and serving of food and ceremonies connected with village life.

The Month
Being equatorial, the climate remains hot and humid for most of the year. The rainy season spans from November to April, with December usually being the wettest month and September the driest. Temperatures range from 26 to 33°C (78–91°F), while humidity hovers between sixty and ninety per cent. While Lombok enjoys refreshingly cool temperatures in the evenings, the wide variety of topographical features gives rise to different microclimates. The island has some of the best surfing waves in the world on spectacularly exotic beaches. Locals all agree that September is the best time for making the most of the east coast's dramatic breakers, while the west coast remains tranquil enough for snorkelling.

King Pacific Lodge

Canada

You can rest assured that from beginning to end, this trip is going to be an expertly orchestrated dream come true. If choosing to stay overnight in Vancouver before heading to the lodge, I would recommend the stylish Fairmont airport hotel for comfort and convenience. During check-in at the airport, a tangible buzz of excitement electrifies the atmosphere as guests introduce themselves to each other. Everyone is keenly anticipating the adventure ahead as you board the plane for the two-hour flight to Prince Rupert in northern British Columbia.

From Prince Rupert, a sixty-minute seaplane journey passes nothing but trees and water. After sweeping over tiers of lakes connected by chalk-streaked waterfalls, the verdant mountainous inlets enclose you like a giant hug as the amphibious plane glides into the numbingly beautiful horseshoe bay of Barnard Harbour. First impressions are always memorable and never more so than here, where a line of healthy smiling faces

waits to welcome you as you step on to this floating platform that promises five-star luxury amid the wilderness. As the previous guests are waved off, sad to be leaving, the plane soars up over the jumping salmon and disappears around the headland, leaving the new arrivals to take stock of what is to be their home for the next few days – hundreds of miles from civilisation.

King Pacific Lodge is truly unique, situated in one of the most awe-inspiring places you can visit on earth. Each year this magnificent floating lodge, owned by Hideo 'Joe' Morita of Sony fame, is tugged all the way from Prince Rupert to the protected cove of Barnard Harbour on Princess Royal Island for the summer months.

Guests are welcomed into the huge ground-floor sitting room-cum-dining room – the hub of activity in the lodge – and gather round the crackling warmth of the log fire. Naturally lit by floor-to-ceiling windows, the space has been carefully furnished with large

leather armchairs and decorated with art solely from the Pacific northwest, reflecting the culture, beauty and diversity of British Columbia. Two Inuit tapestries flank the staircase, while the cream walls are set with paintings of the Spirit Bear, a running wolf and a model of a kayak with a miniature set of equipment made from traditional materials like caribou hide and antler. The lodge rocks so gently that you have to fix your eyes on a point on the horizon to notice it move.

The lodge is surrounded by forests of hemlock and cedar in an area that constitutes twenty-five per cent of the world's remaining temperate rainforest. Some mornings, even before breakfast, you might see bald eagles perched high on a hemlock branch, or a family of silky fur otters cavorting on the floating cedar tree trunks that anchor the lodge in place. The owner and staff are passionately committed to a policy of leaving no trace on the borrowed land and water. The area is also home to bears, wolves, deer and

Cosy bedrooms.   Stunning bathroom views.
(opposite) **Roaring log fire in the sitting room.**

whales, so a complementary relationship has developed between hotel and nature, unlike earlier exploitation that left pitiful scars from logging that are still visible today.

Bedrooms are agreeably minimalist so as not to detract from the allure of the view. Most rooms have king-size beds with handsome wooden headboards, and unfussy corded wall-to-wall carpets with occasional Indian rugs and tapestries. Shoeless comfort is encouraged. Large armchairs and side tables made from fir trees face the view. Having no room keys adds to the open-hearted house party atmosphere, and guests soon find commonalities with their fellow travellers. Slate bathrooms are fully stocked with jars of rose and lavender bath salts and Natura soaps and shampoos in baskets made from rainforest twigs. All around the lodge, vases are filled with lambent red huckleberries and lush local ferns.

All thirty-four staff offer warm, generous hospitality – they genuinely love what they do and delight in sharing the wonders of the region. The lodge is managed by the humorous Ken Beatty, who exacts nothing less than perfectionism from his family of staff. Guests also have the resources of an expert guide to lead kayaking and hiking expeditions and

wildlife viewing. Norman Hann, the lodge's naturalist who is also a qualified high school teacher and national-calibre athlete, brings nature alive, sharing an extensive knowledge of the flora and fauna of British Columbia.

The lodge is located in Git Ga'at First Nations territory and local Hartley Bay guides, such as Darryl Robinson, work side by side with lodge guides and naturalists. Darryl is unfalteringly calm and knowledgeable and adores being paid for what he loves doing. His childhood memories are full of dawn-till-dusk adventures in 'God's Own Country' when every day was spent fishing and whale watching. He's happy to report that whales are now returning in the large numbers he remembers as a youngster.

The 'wellness in the wilderness' ocean-fronted spa is run by Kim Takeuchi. Super-sensitive to your needs, she has a wonderful healing ability to soothe away physical and mental niggles. An ever-evolving menu of treatments changes from season to season and incorporates the expertise of individual therapists. The eighty-five-minute mud and stone wrap treatment is pure bliss, using a therapeutic Casselman mud for detoxification and relaxation. An alternative way to thaw out after being thigh-deep in a river is to jump

into the Jacuzzi, sauna or steam room that overlooks the bay and watch others return.

Meals in this wilderness are always keenly anticipated. Before dinner, drinks are served at seven o'clock with a different tray of canapés each evening. The chefs are totally undaunted by the remoteness of the lodge and make the most of the natural larder on their doorstep, integrating local seafood, mushrooms and wild berries into daily dishes. The fabulous three-course dinners include treats such as porcini braised Trutch Sound halibut with thyme potatoes, organic kale and Edamame beans, followed by steamed squash pudding with chai double cream and caramelised apples. Alternatively you can always ask the chef to prepare the fish you caught that day. On the way up to bed, candlelit trays of petits-fours are placed on the stairs to satisfy any lingering sweet tooth.

Each day boats and helicopters set off from the lodge on a variety of excursions, with guests in Mustang boat attire complete with internal flotation aids and welly boots. Nothing quite compares to observing nature's creatures in the wild – up close. A choice of guided activities includes salt-water and fly-out 'heli' fishing, or watching whales, seals, sea lions, otters and bears.

The Kermode Bear.   **Kayaking in Cameron Cove.**   (opposite) **Luxury in a glorious wilderness.**

In September the rivers are full of pink salmon jostling for position, flipping their tails so hard they catapult out of the water causing a great splashing commotion. They congregate at bends in the river and are easily identifiable as dark shadows. World-class coho fishing awaits in these cold northern waters, whether you're a complete novice or discerning angler looking for fly-fishing in the wilderness of virgin rivers and lakes around the lodge, solely accessible by helicopter. Whatever your catch of the day, be it coho, chinook or pink, your guide will expertly gut it in front of you on the pontoon and have it frozen and vacuum-packed in Styrofoam boxes, ready to go back with you as luggage. What better memento of a trip could you wish for?

The waters around the lodge are known as Whale Channel and are abundant feeding grounds for humpbacks, which follow the salmon run up the rainforest inlets deep into the coastal range. The entrancing practice of 'bubble-net' feeding is a regular sight. Silent circling is followed by pungent jets of steamy spray as massive jaws scoop up the herring and krill desperately splattering on the water. Guests sit mesmerised by their majestic bulk carving slowly in and out of the sea, listening to the bellowing calls echo around the banks of the surrounding islands. Single whales toss and turn waving their fins, suddenly diving deep into the still black waters, and seconds later they breach high into the air exposing an underside covered in molluscs.

Kayaking is easy to master and a delightful way to explore the Cameron Cove inlet – fresh air filling your lungs and sea spray on your lips as you unobtrusively dip your paddle among the giant kelp and the seals and salmon.

The White, Spirit or Kermode bear is a genetically unique member of the black bear family found only on the north coast of British Columbia. A native legend tells how a raven visited the island and made every tenth black bear white to remind its people of the ice age,

and after seeing its comical fishing tricks, you won't stop smiling for a week.

Among some of the most tranquil scenery anywhere on earth, far away from offices, shops, cars, telephones and all the normal trappings of everyday life, the rhythm of time here is dictated by nature. This wilderness provides the ultimate tonic and restores your faith in the world.

The Month

The weather in September is highly changeable, at one minute bright and calm, the next grey and turbulent. The rain, known as liquid gold to the locals, brings ethereal mists that drape the harbour at dawn.

The miraculous salmon run is the anchor of all life in this region and the pivot of the forest eco-system. Each September the salmon return to spawn in the rivers they were born in, and the bears, having finished the berries on higher ground, come down to feed on them. They are easy prey as they pack the streams in huge shoals and the hungry bears catch them with ease, often taking just a single bite from the stomach before selecting another, while bald and golden eagles swoop down to eat the smaller salmon.

October

Çirağan Palace

Istanbul

Turkey stands at the crossroads between Asia and Europe, with Istanbul the dividing line. The river Bosphorus cuts through the city, dividing ancient palace from modern office block: you can stand on one bank and clearly see the buildings on the other – the same city in the same country but on another continent. With a rich, complex history going back more than 2,000 years, Istanbul, once Constantinople, has been the meeting point of three of the world's greatest civilisations: Roman, Byzantine and Ottoman. It was here that the 1,000-year-old Byzantine Empire nourished early Christian roots until replaced by the advent of Islam and the great Ottoman Empire, which stretched from the Atlantic to the Persian Gulf and from Vienna to India.

While Turkey's territories have been slowly whittled away over the centuries, Istanbul is still recognised as the vibrant heart of the nation, with a fabulous heritage of architecture, culture and cuisine that has made the city a world-class tourist destination.

Just as east meets west, the Çirağan Palace, lying on the European shores of the Bosphorus, has succeeded in blending historical tradition with the comfort of modern technology. Staying at the hotel is to feel history coming alive, as this Ottoman palace was once home to the last of the sultans.

Originally built from wood as a summer mansion at the end of the sixteenth century, it was remodelled many times until extravagantly reconstructed in marble for Sultan Abdülaziz in 1857. After the last sultan was deposed during a military takeover, the palace became the new location for parliament to convene. In 1910, after only two months, a fierce fire broke out and thousands of priceless antiques, paintings and books were lost, together with countless vital documents. Following centuries of grandeur, the palace was sadly ruined, left a humble derelict shell with no future. The twentieth century saw it untouched for decades, used as a dumping ground and football pitch, until 1986 when it

was rescued and lovingly restored by the Kempinski Hotel Group. Its reconstruction is a remarkable feat.

The Çirağan Palace is actually two hotels: the restored sultan's palace itself, and an adjoining grand hotel of twentieth-century architecture. Lavish contemporary comfort combined with touches of Ottoman elan dominate the public rooms, which are high-ceilinged and coated in swathes of marble. The new wing has been constructed to complement the scale and design of the original building and, although bigger, it in no way overwhelms the irreplaceable beauty of the palace, whose flamboyant extravagances have been subtly echoed in the new building, which contains most of the 315 rooms.

Bedrooms have the advantage of sliding doors opening on to a spacious balcony directly facing the shores of the Bosphorus; and they enjoy a distinctive rich Ottoman decor of locally hand-woven fabrics and carpets. Decorative frescoes and intricately carved marble

(opposite) **Lavish and flamboyant restoration.** **Swimming on the Bosphorus.**

stonework are found in both the new and the old wings, with spacious marble bathrooms offering plentiful Bulgari toiletries.

You'll certainly eat well at the Çirağan. A spectacular breakfast buffet is presented in the Laledan restaurant, comprising delicacies from around the world – and in the evening a feast of international cuisine including four dishes from seven countries makes decisions almost impossible.

Built within the walls of the sultan's palace, facing the Bosphorus, the Tugra restaurant offers fine Turkish dining at its best, specialising in traditional Ottoman cuisine recreated using authentic recipes from the palace kitchens. French chef Fabrice Cannelle has combined the rich imperial cultural influences and inheritances with modern Turkish cuisine.

The ornate Turkish hammam, which was all that survived the 1910 fire reasonably intact, has been carefully cleaned and authentically restored to its original state, including intricately engraved wall decorations. No longer enjoyed for its original use, it is now reserved as a special venue where hosts can surprise their guests with an eastern fairy-tale setting during intimate dinners.

For an authentic spa experience, the newly renovated Onacua spa area on the ground floor of the hotel offers sauna, Turkish bath, Jacuzzi, massage, solarium, a fully equipped gymnasium and indoor pool.

Outside, the grounds have been groomed to impeccable standards. A huge Ottoman arch – through which many a sultan passed – forms the pièce de résistance, alongside a huge swimming pool (heated in winter to 30°C) spilling out on to the Bosphorus.

Since opening, the hotel has hosted royalty, heads of state, artists and celebrities. Its success lies in its ability to blend its stunning location, requisite grand hotel service and warm Turkish hospitality – indeed, Turkish people are refreshingly friendly and love children.

Needless to say, in this enchanting city there's a plethora of must-do tourist activities, including a trip along the winding twelve-mile channel that separates Asia from Europe, flowing its way towards the Black Sea. The banks of the Bosphorus are scattered with medieval timbered buildings and castles, waterfront palaces and Ottoman mansions. For a longer trip, venture out to the Princes' Islands, ten miles out in the Marmara, for a taste of erstwhile Istanbul where the horse and trap replace the car.

Within close walking distance of the hotel is the harbourside district of Ortakoy. A fascinating area full of seafood restaurants, speciality antiques, ceramic and jewellery shops and at the weekend a colourful street market selling Turkish handicrafts beside the famed Ortakoy Mosque.

Contemporary comfort.   Marble lobby.   (opposite) Istanbul at sunset

Other sightseeing hotspots include the cathedral of St Sophia and the Yerebetan cistern decorated in ancient frescoes and inspiration for centuries of Christian leadership; followed by a visit to the Topkapi Palace. The Blue Mosque is the most prominent in Turkey, and known worldwide as the only mosque with six minarets, famous for the blue Iznik tiles and its striking profile silhouetted against the evening sky.

No visit to Istanbul is complete without a trip to the covered Grand Bazaar. As a thriving crossroads of international trade, Istanbul has long been recognised as a merchant's mecca. All around the entrances to the bazaar a multitude of sights and sounds interlace like the intricately woven carpets found on every corner. Traffic jams accumulate around the clock, but thankfully taxis are plentiful and

cheap. Bargaining in the Grand Bazaar is all part of the entertainment. With 4,000 shops selling leather goods, antiques, jewellery, gold, carpets and ceramics, it's the biggest market in the world. Don't miss the fragrant Spice Bazaar selling fruits, vegetables, flowers and fish.

Istanbul's location has never been more poignant, with one arm reaching out to Asia and the other embracing Europe. Though the sultans have long gone, the Çirağan Palace still breathes elegant luxury, opulence and comfort as a new era of civilisation continues to grow.

The Month
Istanbul has a typical Mediterranean climate, enjoying hot summers and cold winters. By October the feverish heat has turned into

pleasant warmth and the sun's rays cast long shadows across the city. The Çirağan Palace celebrates Turkish Republic Day on 29 October with a lavish banquet in the hotel; additionally there's the Olive Festival from 2 to 10 October; and an international festival celebrating the *gullet*, a traditional Turkish boat.

The Oberoi Vilās

Introduction, India

India is a land of paradox: an embodiment of richness and poverty, opulence and dilapidation, exhilaration and exhaustion, delight and despair. For every wonder and enchantment there lies a bewildering testament to the struggle of its one billion inhabitants. The complexities of life are never more vivid, and every visitor who witnesses subsistence living and extravagant luxury walking hand in hand along the dusty streets experiences the crude workings of human society.

Every sense is tuned to full volume in India. Anywhere else in the world the exotic spectrum of colour would appear gaudy and brash – here it is a natural reflection of the richness of the earth, its people and culture. To the tourist, every street corner provides a memory infused with the colour, smells and noises of life lived to the full.

Some visitors choose to attack India like an assault course, ticking off the sights, while others change their pace and let experiences come to them. Whichever way you choose to enjoy this complex country, rest assured that the following destinations and hotels will enthral and delight you.

Uniquely, I have included four properties in this chapter featuring Rajasthan. India's wealth of culture, particularly throughout this region, makes it impossible to choose between Agra's Taj Mahal, the Amber Fort at Jaipur, Udaipur's Lake and City Palaces, and the tigers of Ranthambore. Some will argue that even here many wonders have been excluded – however, what each of these destinations has in common is a gloriously lavish hotel.

Oberoi's Vilās properties have successfully changed the face of hotels in India forever. Aware that they were going to make a huge impact with their bold architecture in Rajasthan's golden triangle, the designers meticulously thought through the style and concept of each hotel. The result is interiors that totally reflect the lavish resources available from each hotel's own back yard.

The other outstanding component of the Vilās properties is the personalised level of service, summed up by one American guest who stated quite matter-of-factly, 'After a day out sightseeing and shopping I like to feel I'm coming home.' As addictive as the people and noises of the streets can be, it's imperative to be able to escape the chaos and chill out in your palace of serenity away from the threatening intensity of life outside. The seemingly subliminal communication that occurs between you and your butler means that staff are always in the right place at the right time to soothe away the guard you built up to cope with the world going on outside.

The Month

Monsoons occur across India during the summer months between June and September, with particularly heavy rains in July and August. From October to March the cooler winter season offers predictable sunshine and blue skies, with clear air still fresh from the recent rainfall. Across the land, the Hindu festivals of Navarati (dancing), Dussehra and the famous Diwali (lights) are celebrated in October and are a sight not to be missed.

The Oberoi Amarvilās

Agra, India

The city of Agra is recognised across the world for a single building: the Taj Mahal. Sited on the banks of the Yamuna River, 200 kilometres south of Delhi, it was built by Shah Jahan to house the tomb of his beloved wife Mumtaz Mahal, and is universally accepted as the world's most famous monument to love.

Agra has a rich history, reaching its zenith in the mid sixteenth to seventeenth centuries – during Shah Jahan's time – as the capital of the Mughals, during which time art, culture and commerce flourished. The old sector of Agra is still like a medieval city – with unmade narrow lanes bordered with open-fronted shops selling gold, silver and marble handicrafts – and is best experienced from the vantage point of a little rickshaw.

At last there is a hotel in Agra that does justice to its neighbour. Located just 600 metres from the Taj Mahal, set in nine acres of elaborate gardens, pavilions, fountains and reflection pools, The Oberoi Amarvilās has been created to salute the matchless beauty of the building it faces.

You enter through an impressive colonnaded forecourt flanked with marble elephants to the refreshing sound of water spouting forth from the sixty-four carved stone fountains. It took 600 skilled workmen over a year to complete the stonework and carvings throughout Amarvilās. This leads into the lobby dominated by the immense gold-leafed cupola and crystal chandelier, with an eye-catching geometric patterned marble floor and gilded frescoes.

The hotel has been designed in such a way that every bedroom affords a view of the Taj Mahal. Each of the superior deluxe rooms benefits from a private terrace entered through an arched window framing the wondrous view, while the opulent colours and textures of the furnishings are a celebration of it. A large embroidered headboard, wood and marble marquetry side table, teak floors, turquoise silk chairs and hand-embroidered cushions showcase the rich artistic heritage and expertise of the local craftsmen. Additions like the wooden magazine rack and pretty

wooden alarm clock illustrate Oberoi's attention to their guests' comfort.

Opposite the wood-panelled walk-in closet the spacious bathroom has a large bath and separate shower stall finished in Greek marble and turquoise Pilkington glass, with a generous supply of toiletries. The heavy doors are prevented from slamming by silk rope doorstoppers – thoughtful and attractive.

As you gaze from your balcony across the hotel lawns, the Taj Mahal sits like India's very own Sleeping Beauty's Palace behind a lush canopy of banyan trees. From this privileged position with uninterrupted views you notice the changes in colour of the majestic mausoleum as the light varies throughout the day. At dawn the marble has a thick opaque quality that gives it an ethereal quality of peace and holiness. As the sun rises the marble changes from white to a mirror of golden yellow brilliance, sparkling as rays of light catch the millions of inlaid gems. At dusk the marble looks as though it has been swathed in pink chiffon.

(opposite) **Spa Suite.** **Bedroom.**

In all the Vilās properties, the food is as exotic as the sights. Senior Kitchen Executive Siddharth Chowdhry can be seen in action working in his show kitchen behind a soundproofed window overlooking a corner of the Esphahân restaurant, which specialises in Awadhi and north Indian cuisine. Each night musicians perform on a dais surrounded by red sandstone and Greek Thassos marble, while fastidious gourmets tuck into wonderful *thalis* served on colossal silver platters.

The spa, operated by the celebrated Banyan Tree group, has maximised its unique position and has converted three suites into special treatment rooms with a view like no other. Lying in a warm scented bath full of rose petals, overlooking the Taj Mahal, you feel you're part of a fairy-tale picture book. The non-clinical programmes for relaxation and beauty include an extensive menu of Ayurvedic treatments incorporating the principles of holistic health maintenance, herbal treatments and aromatherapy. If you're planning a tour of Rajasthan and starting here, it is definitely worth making an appointment with the Banyan Tree spa therapists who will plan a treatment programme based on your itinerary and needs.

The heat treatment rooms include steam and sauna rooms next to the gym. The spa area has direct access to the hotel's gardens and swimming pool – a stunning eighty-foot basin of water with a colonnaded annexe surrounded by terraces.

I strongly recommend you ask the concierge at Amarvilās to arrange for one of their erudite guides to escort you around the several places of interest within Agra. The Agra Fort is particularly well worth visiting. Originally known as Akbarabad, it was built by Emperor Akbar to symbolise the great Mughal imperial culture he had created.

Situated on the west bank of the Yamuna River, its imposing red sandstone ramparts form a crescent along the riverfront and encompass an enormous complex of buildings.

Akbar's love of aesthetics was inherited by his grandson, Shah Jahan, who embellished the buildings he commissioned with tons of marble on a scale unmatched to this day. Devastated by his beloved wife's death, he decided to build her a monument of 'poetry in marble' – the Taj Mahal. It is only up close that the brilliant combination of shining white marble, coloured mosaic and precious and semi-precious stone inlay and latticework can be truly admired.

The utter privilege of enjoying the peaceful beauty of the Taj Mahal at any time, and in a style that Shah Jahan himself would savour, makes an interlude at Amavilās totally irresistible. If you want to leave nothing to chance, there is simply nowhere else to stay in Agra.

The Oberoi Vanyavilās

Ranthambhore, India

The majestic Indian tiger is the fundamental reason why travellers come to this remote corner of south-western Rajasthan. Sightings are definitely on the increase here in the 300-square-kilometre Ranthambhore National Park, which nestles between the Vindhya and Aravalli mountain ranges. Until recently there's been nowhere enticing to stay – but now India's first luxury wildlife resort has been erected in twenty acres of orchards abutting the park.

Each day new guests are met at the hotel gates by two Indian elephants – the eighteen-year-old Mala (meaning Garland) and her fifteen-year-old companion Laxmi (name of a Hindu god) as they raise their trunks to signify their welcome. Stepping through the huge carved wooden door of the *haveli* or mansion into the lobby, guests are greeted with fresh hot towels and a fruit punch. Colourful frescoes of peacocks – India's national bird – decorate the walls and brightly attired staff escort you past the elegant library to your air-conditioned 'tent', the term used liberally in this case!

Vanyavilās is a resort hotel encompassing twenty-five such tents, which meander round a small lake below the steep escarpment of the Aravalli cliffs. Most of the tents are enclosed within an adobe-walled garden surrounded with flowering trees and bushes, ensuring privacy for sunbathers. Here you can rest on teak chaise-longues under sweet-smelling frangipani bushes that overlook the mango groves towards the park.

Inside, the teak floors are covered in tiger-striped rugs while a lavish four-poster bed, littered with jungle-print cushions and colourful throws, stands under a canvas ceiling embossed with tigers woven from golden thread – you never forget why you're here. Spacious bathrooms have roll-top baths, teak-lined dressing closets and double vanities with all the usual toiletries.

Tiger sightings are a thrilling, unforget-table experience, but four hours of chasing tracks can leave you ready for a bit of pampering in the spa. The personalised holistic therapies offered at Vanyavilās are based on Ayurvedic and western techniques and incorporate local herbs, flowers and spices. It's always fun to try the local cures, and the invigorating herbal pouch massage followed by a bath in neem leaves is a great way to chill out before dinner.

Executive Chef Saurav Banerjee enjoys cooking uncomplicated dishes that bring out all the natural flavours of the ingredients, and his menu has a rustic theme reflecting its forest location. He'll be only too delighted to show you round his impressive kitchen garden where immaculate rows of organic vegetables and herbs line up soldier-fashion under various fruit trees.

You can eat anywhere on the estate, but generally meals are served in either the frescoed air-conditioned restaurant or outside in the pretty courtyard, heated by a constantly burning log fire.

(opposite) **Frescoed restaurant.**   **Animal-print luxury.**   **Courtyard restaurant.**

At only twenty-nine, the dedicated and beautiful Lincy Issac is the youngest person ever to become a general manager at Oberoi. Running Vanyavilās is her dream come true, reflected in the way she manages her seventy-five staff – that's three members of staff for each room – and the top-notch service they provide.

At seven o'clock each evening, the eminent naturalist Mr Fateh Singh, known as the 'tiger man' (India's answer to Sir David Attenborough), makes an hour-long presentation on the flora and fauna found in the reserve. The next morning you leave before breakfast to see if your luck is in. If the tigers and leopards prove to be elusive, you will definitely encounter various other animals that coexist with the giant cats, including peacocks by the dozen, partridge, monkeys, crocodile, exotic birds, many kinds of deer and, if you're lucky, the adorable sloth bear.

In the middle of the forest the mighty Ranthambhore Fort lies like a legendary lost city and stories of heroism and fierce battles abound, stretching back a thousand years.

When not out on a game drive, you can relax by the pool, take an elephant ride, or walk through the grounds to the lofty watchtower affording far-reaching views of the park. From below, the intricate tracery of the indigenous Dhok trees patterns the blue skies, while the distinctive calls of green parakeets echo through the air.

Ranthambhore is best described as Kipling's *Jungle Book* come to life. It's been loved by the tiger-hunting Maharajas of Jaipur for centuries – but today it's a refuge for all who inhabit or visit its sanctuary.

October is a beautiful time of year to visit the forest because it's still lush and green after soaking up the monsoon rains. Animal sightings are less frequent because water holes are still widely dispersed, but days are hot and nights are cool and the flourishing bird life is at its finest.

The Oberoi Rajvilās

Jaipur, India

For pure scenic splendour, architectural wealth, music, dance and handicrafts, Jaipur offers a depth, quality and variety unmatched in India. Commonly referred to as the Pink City, it gained its nickname in 1876, when walls were universally coated in pink to celebrate the visit of the Prince of Wales (the future King Edward VII).

The story of Rajvilās begins with the painstaking restoration of a private Rajasthani fort at Naila near Jaipur. P. R. S. Oberoi, founder of the eponymous hotel group, who enjoyed the fort as a secondary residence, was encouraged by its popularity with his private guests to search for a similar property for his group. A *haveli*, or mansion, was found a comfortable five miles from the Pink City in an area of pastoral beauty – and the rest, as they say, is history.

Located in thirty-two acres of landscaped gardens, among orchards, decorative pools and fountains, Rajvilās is an evocative golden fort in an oasis of calm luxury. Guests enter through huge, elaborately decorated, brass-clad doors, each eleven feet wide, into the haven of gardens. At the centre an ancient Hindu temple is surrounded by moats filled with flowering water lilies and lotus blooms, interspersed with turreted pergolas entwined with colourful bougainvillaea, swathes of emerald lawns, neem trees, desert palms, beds of jasmine and fragrant herb gardens. It's reassuring to see that the temple has retained its sacred purpose and remains the spiritual heart of the hotel. Throughout the day staff come and go with their offerings and prayers, while early-morning yoga sessions are actively encouraged within the precincts of the shrine.

Lying to the west of the temple, the main swimming pool, lined with Jaipuri pottery tiles, is surrounded by multi-levelled terraces, sun lounges and tasselled umbrellas, flanked by white pillars and domed temples. Over-looking the pool, the spa is housed in the original *haveli*, and offers Ayurvedic-inspired holistic treatments for both beauty and relaxation. The eight treatment rooms and four spa suites are decorated in hand-painted frescoes and grouped around a bubbling whirlpool in an open-air courtyard. In addition to the treatment rooms, there's a steam room, sauna, Jacuzzi and state-of-the-art gymnasium that overlooks a traditional Mughal herb garden – a replica of the gardens at the famous Amber Fort. Further along, a jogging track leads to two floodlit tennis courts, croquet greens and a mini-putting course.

Accommodation of various sorts circles the temple and lotus pond. Most of the fifty-four bedrooms have been grouped in clusters of four or six around tranquil courtyards, in addition to three romantic villas with private pools and thirteen Rajasthani tented rooms decorated along similar lines to those found at Vanyavilās. All the courtyard rooms have a regal teak four-poster bed, an appealing cushioned window seat and an exotic sunken white Italian marble bath overlooking private walled gardens.

Travellers today have discerning palates and are increasingly spoilt for choice by the

Surya Mahal restaurant. **Courtyard bedroom.** (opposite) **Lobby.**

variety and quality of cuisine around the world. General manager Paul Jones is therefore delighted that the chefs at Rajvilās have succeeded in creating a light, fusion style of cooking, taking traditional elements from various Asian countries. The chic Surya Mahal restaurant offers a menu of exceptional class, featuring the best of both international and Indian cuisine including spectacular local *thalis*. On balmy evenings, a pleasant alternative is to dine in the courtyard under a starlit sky, entertained by traditional performances of Indian music and dance against the dramatic backdrop of the fort.

All around Rajasthan you find local people dressed in extraordinary fabrics and costumes, carrying them off with grace and panache. Indian fashion designer Tarun Tahliani has brought this striking flavour to the Rajvilās through the lavish uniforms and headdresses worn by the staff, reflecting the colourful history and culture of the region.

Rajvilās provides the perfect setting from which to plan your daily excursions to the exotic palaces, forts, festivals and teeming bazaars around Jaipur. The hotel benefits

from a strong association with local craft and culture, and will put together a list of shops and sights tailored to your interests.

Surrounded by a high wall known as the Sarahad, the spectacular City Palace is the residence of the former ruling family of Jaipur, occupying one-seventh of the city centre. It reflects a combination of Rajput beauty, Mughal spaciousness and English linear planning. The Hawa Mahal, or Palace of Winds, is a trompe l'oeil in masonry, appearing to be part of the palace – in fact it is all façade, an elaborate palace exterior complete with 953 windows. It's a fascinating maze of corridors and resting points once used by royal women to peep out and observe the city below.

The outer courtyard, now a museum, holds two huge silver *gangajalis*, or urns, capable of holding 1,600 gallons of liquid each. They were used by the present maharaja's grandfather for his trip to Queen Victoria's Diamond Jubilee – he didn't trust the English water so filled the huge urns with sufficient Ganga water to cleanse himself.

There are few sights in Rajasthan that match the majesty and grandeur of the great

Amber Fort. From the twelfth to the eighteenth centuries, Amber was one of the most important of all Rajput cities. The seventeenth-century fort and its courtly gardens occupies a steep hillside inside eleven miles of defensive wall. After passing through a series of five protective gates, you reach the first courtyard of the Raj Mahal, home to the green marble-pillared temple to Kali, goddess of war, and the stunning Mirror Palace.

Artisans from all over the country were invited to work in the city – a request that has left a legacy of expert craftsmanship in hand-blocked textiles, jewellery and pottery. The city's flourishing commercial activities offer a metropolis of unparalleled retail opportunities, attracting designers, artists and discerning shoppers from across the world.

Staff at the hotel can arrange safaris on beautifully decorated elephants, as well as horse or elephant polo, camel-back riding, or an unforgettable evening of entertainment at a Bollywood movie. At the end of it all you can return to your comfort zone and step back into the romantic luxury of Jaipur's most opulent residence – Rajvilās.

The Oberoi Udaivilās

Udaipur, India

Udaipur means the 'city of sunrise'. It is one of India's most romantic and enchanting cities, set in the lush oasis of the Girwa Valley surrounded by the Aravalli mountain range on the edge of Lake Pichola. Capital of the old kingdom of Mewar, one of the longest surviving dynasties in the world, legend has it that the royal Rajput rulers are descended directly from the sun god himself. Through the ages the Maharanas of Mewar have continued to embrace the golden sun as their royal insignia, and it remains a recurring motif throughout the region.

The beguiling tapestry of temples, forts, cenotaphs, palaces and lakes is a ravishing setting for India's newest palace hotel, The Oberoi Udaivilās. Guests arrive from the opposite shore of the lake aboard one of the hotel's elegant launches to a private jetty in the grounds. Spread over thirty acres of landscaped lawns and lakeside gardens, the hotel is a romantic extravaganza of courtyards, walkways, arches, domes and alcoves. Cool reflecting pools and rippling fountains soften the intensity of the midday heat, while at dusk its vast external canvas has something of a lambent quality as its hue changes with the fading force of the sun's rays.

All the reception rooms have an ambience of regal splendour, embellished with hand-painted frescoes, intricate mirrors and beautiful works of art from around the region. Next to the lobby is the Candle Room, a miniature Sheesh Mahal or glass palace, where a circular table is covered in dozens of candles creating flickering shadows across the *thekri*-covered walls. The hotel has nine swimming pools (five of them private), and in the gardens there are endless opportunities for picnics while enjoying the fairytale vista across the lake.

Bedrooms are ornately decorated in darkly polished woods, hand-knotted carpets, Rajasthani quilts and rich silks. White marble bathrooms with Victorian-style roll-top baths face the lake-side view. Opt for one of the rooms with a recessed courtyard and semi-private infinity-edge pool – you can step from your bedroom's outdoor dining pavilion into the refreshing waters of the ribbon-shaped pool that wraps its way around the southern terrace without interrupting the view of the lake and palaces.

Meals are generally taken in either of the two restaurants: Suryamahal, the main daytime dining room; or in Udaimahal, the speciality Indian restaurant decorated to represent the night sky. On hot summer evenings the adjoining Chandni restaurant is perfect for al fresco dinners, which are accompanied by live performances of music and dance.

For relaxation, Udaivilās has a luxurious two-storey spa (managed by Banyan Tree) and a swimming pool that overlooks the lake to the mountains beyond. All eight therapy suites have their own bath, steam and sauna, and the synchronised massage given by the Thai-trained staff is the best in the world: two therapists use simultaneous rhythmic movements as you are anointed with herbal oils from head to toe – an experience that leaves you walking on air.

(opposite) **Lake Udaipur.** **Rural Rajasthan.**

While you have the energy, tear yourself away from the lake view – there's even more beauty to appreciate further afield. One of the biggest attractions – literally – is the City Palace, the home of the Maharana of Mewar. Although it has a single façade, the palace is composed of four major palaces and several minor palaces. Entered through a triple arch, the gate leads to a series of courtyards, narrow corridors and gardens. By far the most popular attraction is the seventeenth-century Mor Chowk or Peacock Courtyard, which derives its name from the inlaid glass mosaics of peacocks on its walls.

The Crystal Gallery in Fateh Prakesh overlooks the great Durbur Hall and houses a rare collection of Osler's crystal including glass chairs, tables and a bed ordered from England by Maharana Sajjan Singh.

Dominating the city's skyline is Sajjan Garh, also known as the Monsoon Palace, located at the top of a hill called Bansdara overlooking Lake Pichola. Maharana Sajjan Singh built the palace in the seventeenth-century as an observatory for monsoon clouds, which on a clear day can be spotted as far as Chittaurgarh, over a hundred kilometres away. Sadly, it stands abandoned but remains a perfect spot to watch the sun disappear over the stunning Aravalli mountain range.

In the centre of Lake Pichola lies a small island called Jag Mandir. Prince Khurram (later to become the great Shah Jahan) famously took refuge in a building here, and was deeply moved by the symmetry of its dome which later inspired the most famous dome in the world: of course, the Taj Mahal.

Sitting on the terrace of your dream palace, it's very easy to understand just how this setting stirred him.

In October the skies are clear again and the hills are touched with pink in the evenings. The colourful Dussehra celebrations are in progress – looked on by the spirits of Radha and Krishna.

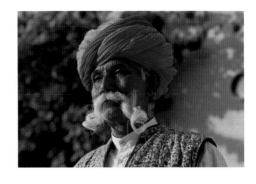

The Sharrow Bay Hotel

England

The Sharrow Bay Hotel is an English tale of success and endurance – and something of a legend. Reputed to be the world's original country house hotel, it is situated in the Lake District National Park of Cumbria, among scenery that is unrivalled in England. The main house, of soft grey Lakeland stone, is situated along a cul-de-sac, on a promontory on the eastern edge of Lake Ullswater. With its low angled roof and wide eaves, the overall façade is reminiscent of a Swiss chalet or an Italian villa. A boathouse and a private jetty are the only other constructions that lie along the half mile of private shore – where privacy and peace reign supreme.

The concept of the country house hotel was created in 1948 by the late Francis Coulson, who was then joined in his scheme by his partner, Brian Sack. Francis first saw the house advertised in the *Manchester Guardian* as 'a mansion on the edge of Ullswater with twelve acres of grounds' – and decided that it was the answer to his dream. My mother first visited the house when she

was only ten and can well remember the fascinating, collections of porcelain, books, china, portraits and landscapes. The eccentric decor has toned down a little, but the unique flamboyant spirit is still very much alive.

The staff comprises mainly local people, many having trained and worked at the hotel for several decades; and a good helping of French folk, working mainly in the restaurants. Today's proprietor is the twinkly-eyed Nigel Lightburn, loved by Brian as 'the son I never had', whose thirty-six years of service is evidence of his passion for the property. His extraordinary attentiveness and full-time presence are exceptional in today's world of anonymous management, and symptomatic of his love affair with this stretch of the Lakes. There's definitely something different going on here and it's highly contagious.

Guests are welcomed at the front door with warm smiles, and a glass of sherry awaits while you sign the visitors' book, before admiring the alluring view across to the Martindale Fells from the picture window in

the drawing room. 'Take a breath and listen to the quietness,' suggests Nigel. One hears a cuckoo in the distance, a bee humming somewhere nearby and a cork popping from a bottle of wine. Other than that, pure silence.

The main building, still brimming with a diverse assortment of antiques and the scent of fresh flowers, now houses six individually refurbished double-bedded suites and one single, with characteristic names such as 'Marian', 'Pinky' and 'Regina'. Two newly appointed ground-floor Garden Suites, incorporating the Cottage, which was Francis and Brian's home for fifteen years, have spacious wardrobes, luxurious soft furnishings of damask and silk, and private views across the garden and lake.

A mile down the lane towards Howtown is Bank House, a secluded annexe to the main house, enjoying uninterrupted and intimate views of the fells and lake, popular with people wanting a little extra privacy. A converted Elizabethan farmhouse, it has two sitting rooms overlooking the fells and lake;

Bank House.   (opposite) **Bank House Refectory.**

seven bedrooms and a very unusual refectory (with the fireplace and much of the furniture from Warwick Castle) used for breakfast and afternoon teas. Guests staying at Bank House are chauffeured between the two properties in a people carrier to avoid any worry about levels of intoxication, although the hearty will enjoy the walk back under the stars – in the absence of any light pollution, relishing the heavens at their most dazzling.

A profusion of 'cherubs' throughout the estate is a flamboyant touch. Found in all shapes and sizes, they grace the menus, lamps, walls, pictures, sculptures and garden statuettes, providing a deliciously amusing and eccentric flavour round every corner.

Each night guests gather in the drawing room or conservatory for an aperitif and a leisurely perusal of the lengthy menu. Deciding is almost torturous. An extensive wine list accompanies the menu, including both old and new world vintages, and a helpful visit from the sommelier completes pre-dinner business. The gastronomic delight of its guests has always been an important ingredient of the Sharrow Bay experience, featuring traditional British dishes based on Francis and Brian's philosophy of 'the gentle art of cooking'. Today's head chefs, Johnnie Martin and Colin Akrigg, both protégés of Francis, serve six-course feasts including such tasty delights as pig's trotters

filled with pork shank and wild mushrooms on pease pudding with Madeira sauce, followed by Sharrow fruit sorbets and the most delectable choice of desserts, which are displayed like an artist's easel.

Much to the delight of the management, mobile phones are unable to get a signal, allowing guests to escape from unsolicited interruptions. Breaking with current trends, there's no gym or spa: 'You can go to the gym on Monday,' says Nigel. 'What would you rather be looking at, your cellulite in a room of mirrors, or that view?' he ponders. The guests returning year after year know their preference. In fact it's so quiet you can literally hear the peace, allowing a complete

break from today's manic lifestyle and the rare opportunity to stop and simply take stock.

Unlike Lake Windermere, Ullswater has no motorised water-sports. Instead, guests can go boating, fishing, riding and, of course, walking or climbing. One of the most breath-taking walks in the Lakeland is the six-mile stroll along the south-western edge of Ullswater to Glenridding at the foot of the Helvellyn range – returning in leisurely fashion on *The Lady of the Lake*, the elegant Ullswater steamer. Penrith, seven miles to the east, is full of tempting shops for consumer therapy or a bit of golf at the base of the fells. Sharrow is also within easy distance for a visit to the homes of William Wordsworth, John Ruskin and Beatrix Potter, or one of the numerous sites of archaeological interest.

Fifty-six years on, the Sharrow Bay is going from strength to strength, obstinately breaking the mould of consumer whim and changing only very subtly with the times, always aiming to maintain its unique character and ambience. Total tranquillity wrapped in luxury: the perfect tonic for the city-stressed. The fact that it has retained its reputation for so long is testimony to the rare magic of the setting and quality of hospitality. I look forward with anticipation to seeing what the next few decades have in store for visitors.

The Month

The Lake District... Beatrix Potter, daffodils, fells, Wordsworth and mint-cake are what first come to mind – all of which can be enjoyed the year round (apart from the daffodils for which April is the best month). However, one month in particular seems to resonate with the full spectrum of nature's wonders at the Sharrow Bay. Late October greets sleepy eyes with a heavy carpet of frost, and at five o'clock in the morning the lake rests like polished glass before the thermals begin to rise. Opposite the lake, the view to Hallyn Fell is a spectacular kaleidoscope of colour, comprising over a hundred species of trees in the old wood. Piercing shafts of autumn light catch the canopy of foliage as it metamorphoses into a dense blaze of oranges and reds. Carpets of bracken line the footpaths, virtually untrodden now, with only an occasional passer-by. As summer draws to an end the clear autumn light brings surprising but welcome warmth as the days shorten. The crowds have long departed and the stillness reigns once again.

November

Alvear Palace Hotel

Buenos Aires

Argentina is a country of wildly dramatic geographical contrast. To the east are immense plains, while the Andes mountain range dominates the west. Tierra del Fuego and the lake region, forests and glaciers of Patagonia lie to the south, and in the north are the spectacular Iguazú Falls and dramatic tropical rainforest.

The nation's capital, Buenos Aires, is no less dramatic; a city with a unique style that interweaves the glamour and elegance of its European influences with its essential Latin American spirit. Football is the national obsession – streets are full of boys of all ages wearing their team's colours and practising their footwork.

Standing in the heart of the Recoleta district, the Alvear Palace Hotel is a fine reflection of the country's diversity and grace. Conceived during the so-called *belle époque* before the First World War, it stands as a symbol of that theatrical era. After ten years of construction the doors finally opened in 1932 inviting

guests into a grand building standing eleven storeys high.

The style of the interior is archetypal French of the Louis XIV to Louis XVI period, and it is sumptuously furnished with reproductions of renowned French decorative art. The design was conceived by Dr De Miero, a local entrepreneur and social grandee, aided by Valentín Brodsky, a young architect, who designed the façade with dreams of the building hosting beautiful fairy-tale events.

By the mid twentieth century the hotel had become dated and tired, until in 1984 a group of Argentine businessmen bought it with a view to undertaking significant renovation. The original style has been totally respected, and today the restored Alvear Palace stands resurrected in her former glory as Buenos Aires' undisputed grand dame.

All 210 rooms, half of which are suites, are elegantly decorated in Empire and Louis XV style. They boast deep-pile carpets, chintzy draped windows overlooking the streets of

Recoleta, and beds dressed in starched Frette Egyptian linen with piles of squidgy pillows. Nearly all of the bathrooms have a Jacuzzi, and on the fine marble surfaces sit toiletries by Hermès de Paris – exclusive to Argentina. Each floor has a dedicated butler available at the touch of a button, who will organise for your clothes to be pressed as soon as you arrive. Rooms of all standards have a comfortable sitting area and a large writing desk decorated with fresh flowers and baskets of seasonal fruit replaced daily. Other ingenious touches include the use of a cellular phone that works anywhere in the city and is recharged by your butler each night.

The Alvear offers a number of elaborate dining options, including the popular airy L'Orangerie, known as a traditional place to meet in Buenos Aires for the magnificent buffet breakfast or Sunday brunch. Next to the restaurant is the Jardin d'Hiver, decorated with vibrant plants and flowers, full of trays piled high with tempting patisseries at tea time.

Elegant suite.   The Orangerie.   (opposite) La Bourgogne.

For pastry lovers, the 'Alvear Tea' has become a local classic.

A buzzing *fin de siècle* bar, chock-a-block with mahogany and leather furniture, is filled to the rafters with champagne, wine, a fine selection of cognacs, single malt whiskies and Cuban cigars – a perfect spot for an aperitif or quick snack.

La Bourgogne is commonly regarded as the best restaurant in Buenos Aires. It offers exquisite French cuisine created by French chef Jean Paul Bondoux, who delights demanding gourmets with Argentina's famous steaks cooked in the rotisserie grill. Unlike the rest of the hotel, the decor is contemporary with minimalist cream and white furnishings, and spot lighting in preference to chandeliers. La Cave, the restaurant's former wine cellar, is a good option for an informal country-style meal featuring a regional French menu, also prepared by Jean Paul Bondoux.

Located on the second floor, the hotel's health club has a small indoor heated swimming pool, sauna and gymnasium with computerised equipment for aerobic workouts with the guidance of specialised instructors. After your day's sightseeing, there's a highly skilled Indian lady who gives superlative relaxing massages.

The hotel prides itself on its level of individualised customer service provided by its 400 professional and committed staff, all of whom enjoy ongoing training. It's no surprise that the Alvear Palace Hotel has won worldwide recognition and innumerable awards.

Stepping outside the front door of the hotel, the Recoleta district is a refined neighbourhood with ample parks and wide, tree-lined avenues flanked by elegant architecture. If you were led blindfolded to a street corner you'd swear you were in Europe – probably Paris. Considered the cultural centre of the city, Recoleta is home to dozens of elegant restaurants, bars, discothèques, outdoor shows, a cinema complex and a great handicrafts fair that opens at weekends.

The Recoleta Cemetery is definitely worth a visit for its ornate architectural monuments and vaults. More than seventy have been declared national historic monuments, including that of the illustrious and much-loved national heroine Eva Perón. In the same area crossing Libertador Avenue lies the National Museum of Fine Arts, the impressive Law School buildings and the National Library.

Tango at Esquina Carlos Gardel.   La Boca.

Buenos Aires is full of attractive neighbourhoods. After an extensive process of renovation Palermo is a favourite place for bohemians and intellectuals involved in the arts and literature. Nearby Palermo Soho is packed with contemporary clothes boutiques and interior design shops; while Palermo Hollywood is a gastronomic centre with more than forty bars and restaurants. With a profusion of young and creative chefs, you'll find plentiful ethnic, Mediterranean and international cuisine, and the district is packed with tapas bars in the courtyards of old houses.

San Telmo is one of the oldest neighbourhoods in the city, originally inhabited by Buenos Aires' wealthiest families. Among the narrow streets are the Orthodox Russian church, La Defensa Alley and Colonel Manuel Dorrego Square, famous for its Sunday antiques market.

Whatever you choose to do during the day, make time in the evening for a celebration of the tango – that fusion of cultures and sounds born in the melting pot of Buenos Aires. Carlos Gardel's Tango Theatre provides a dramatic place to dine as you watch a thrilling performance telling the history of the ribald lyrics and sinuous movements that have morphed into a global phenomenon. You'll want to tango all the way back to the Alvear.

The Month

November is the middle of spring in the southern hemisphere, and the ideal time to visit Argentina's capital before the heat of summer arrives (from mid December to February). Each November, both locals and visitors alike flock to soak up the culture as they watch and dance the tango at the World

Tango Championships and accompanying festival held throughout the city. The Argentine Open Polo Championships are held mid-month and, just outside the city in San Antonio de Areco, the Día de la Tradición, the country's largest gaucho festival, is held annually in November.

Hotel de Larache
explora en Atacama

Chile

Deserts normally conjure up images of desolate landscapes, parched sandy dunes rolling towards an ever-distant horizon. The idea of a hotel resort being built in such a destination seems highly unlikely. The reality of the explora en Atacama in northern Chile couldn't be more startling.

Wherever you live in the world, it's probably going to be a long journey to San Pedro en Atacama – and explora certainly make no excuses for their remoteness. Flying westwards over South America, a white line on the horizon stretches from north to south as far as the eye can see – the Andes, tipped with snow even in midsummer. Calama is a two-hour flight due north of Santiago. During the flight the terrain gradually changes from row upon row of lime-green vines punctuated with bizarre circular crop patterns to a more arid landscape. As the snow-capped mountains turn a ruddy brown, the fields disappear to be replaced by the lunar scenery of the Atacama Desert. Dried-up ravines are interrupted by occasional oases hugging a valley delta, and

colours mutate to grey sandy-brown with tints of ochre. You can hardly believe that there can be any form of civilisation in this unforgiving barrenness.

During the seventy-five-minute drive from Calama, the constant change in topography is even more amazing as colours alter round each corner. The increase in altitude causes your ears to pop continually – at 2,500 metres above sea level, the air feels thinner but unbelievably pure.

As the road turns into the oasis of San Pedro, a crossroads of ancient trade routes, the tarmac runs out and the bumpy last mile brings you into the stable courtyard of the Hotel de Larache. Views are breathtaking. A line of volcanoes stretches across the horizon towards Bolivia. Most guests head straight for a swim in one of the four tinglingy cold pools designed by the architects to reflect the irrigation channels of San Pedro – followed by a sauna or hot Jacuzzi in their bathroom.

Situated in the middle of the world's driest desert, the hotel has been designed, equipped

and organised to ensure that you can rest, contemplate, explore, or just marvel at the surroundings. Its ethos is to allow you exposure to the fragility of its remote beauty while sustaining local traditions that have respectfully preserved the quality of the environment for centuries.

Tall grasses and ornamental pepper and carob trees shade the grounds around the hotel. At the heart a triangular courtyard connects bedrooms via ramped walkways leading towards the elevated restaurant, lounge and bar. Everywhere the architecture evokes an estancia feel designed to fit in with the natural world and ethnicity of the Atacama.

Interiors have been decorated in an indigenous style with brightly coloured furniture, wickerware and tapestries crafted by local artisans. Huge deep sofas draped in rugs face the eastern skies while Bolivian slate floors, cypress-wood ceilings and walls hung with colourful Chilean antique rugs echo the rich desert hues.

Once in your bedroom the silence is

(opposite) **Arid walking terrain.**   **Interiors reflect the rich desert hues.**

deafening – with no television to drown its purity. All fifty rooms have a mesmerising twenty-foot-wide panoramic view of the volcanoes that dominate the eastern sky – hinting at the proximity of the Altiplano. The overbearing presence of Licancabur (translated as 'Mountain of the People') is deceptive as it is actually fifty kilometres away. In the bathroom abundant supplies of water pours out from a monsoon-like shower head filling the deep Jacuzzi bath fed by the hotel's own well (and then used to irrigate the fields – saving any guilt complex). You can lie in the bath for hours on end just staring out at the eerie Martian terrain.

Despite its remote location, the cuisine both in the hotel and while on excursions is scrumptious, combining fresh local and international ingredients and techniques. Guests eat together in the bright dining room or on the terrace overlooking Licancabur. Lunch typically features national favourites such as conger eel or Serrano ham, washed down with a palatable dry Chilean Chardonnay from one of the owner's vine-yards. The bar is the perfect spot for an aperitif while watching sunsets so dramatic

that even the staff stop what they're doing to stand and gaze.

An adobe-walled hut lit with candles and scented with fresh garden herbs is an ambrosial location for reiki, reflexology or a massage after a day in the desert. The gentleness of Yilia's whispering in your ear to turn over, and her warm parting hug and kiss leave you with a glow in your heart.

The key reason for visiting explora is the sophisticated menu of inimitable exploration over this otherworldly geology. Every evening guides mingle with you as you sip your cocktail to plan the next day's outing, which ranges from easy-going photo safaris to vigorous all-day hikes. Among the choices are challenging or unhurried horseback rides; sunset saunters over a barren salt lake; hiking to hot springs nestling in a swarded gorge where you can bathe while sipping Pisco Sours; or an intoxicating two-day climb to the summit of a 6,000-metre volcano.

The exhilarating two-hour Kari gorge walk is perfect while you acclimatise – taking you over salt deposits, along cliff-edge paths, sliding down giant sand dunes, through two caves and deep into innumerable ravines

where the only noise to be heard is the distinctive cracking in the salt rocks.

For a sunset phenomenon, take the trip to the small village of Toconao with its ancient chapel and quaint arts and crafts shops packed with alpaca cardigans. From here the road continues on forever like a hazy mirage further and further into the Salar de Atacama. What a magical, mystical place. Ten thousand years ago it was a vibrant lake fed by the rivers descending from the surrounding volcanoes and mountains. Today it's a dead saltpan. Lying right on the Tropic of Capricorn, the bizarre brackish formations extend over thousands of kilometres, attracting hundreds of majestic flamingos. As the sun sets over the volcanoes the softness in the air makes you feel curiously happy – local guides tell guests that no one ever gets depressed up here due to the high levels of lithium and other minerals in the Atacama.

Watching the dawn rise over El Tatio – the world's largest geyser field – is another must. The strange mineral formations and spouting clouds of steam, as much as ten metres high, feel truly supernatural. It's like standing on the lid of a boiling pressure cooker waiting for

Volcanic backdrop. **El Tatio.** (opposite) **San Pedro.**

it to let off steam. The air is freezing but all around brooks bubble with water at scalding temperatures as giant cauldrons erupt, hissing thousands of litres of smoky steam into the freezing morning air.

The steppe landscape of this area, bordering Bolivia's Altiplano region, is characterised by its ability to resist the challenges posed by its extreme altitude. Around El Tatio the only vegetation is lime-green tufts of grass and lichen interspersed by large boulders. A drive further down turns into a desert wildlife safari as groups of shy vicunas graze with their backs turned ready to flee; and ravines are popular drinking holes for South American rhea and flocks of Andean geese.

Returning closer to the hotel, the narrow rocky descent to the Baños de Puritama passes aptly named candelabro and obelisk-formed cactus that are over five hundred years old. Pure bliss awaits. After the extreme aridity of the desert the natural pools heated by steam vents ease your spirit back into a

mood of cosseted civilisation. You'll want to bath here every day, massaging your shoulders under the warm waterfall as you stare through the crystal clear waters.

After all the activity, a gentle afternoon hack on one of the stable's thoroughbreds is a delightful way to orientate yourself around San Pedro – peering over the adobe walls on to the vegetable plots of the local houses.

Expertly run by Englishman Paul Rodwell and his Spanish wife Noemí, whose aim it is to ensure unforgettable memories, explora is so much more than a hotel. It opens a door to experience the remote beauty of the desert, providing water, food, shelter and shade from scorching sun, permitting an ephemeral but intimate encounter with nature where survival would otherwise be the only imperative. Its geology is a feast for the eyes, its people are warm and hospitable, and it provides a rare privilege to experience the harsh but numbing beauty of one of the world's rawest natural territories.

The Month

The climate is magnificent throughout the year, with more than ninety per cent of the days being radiant. Although there is no perfect time to enjoy Chile, the best is during early summer when evenings are comfortably cool and days have not yet reached the scorching levels of midsummer, necessitating a midday siesta. The busiest tourist season is from December to February, but even then it's hardly what you'd call crowded.

Quark Expeditions

Antarctica

The largest wilderness on earth, Antarctica is also the coldest, driest and windiest. With its ground permanently frozen for half a mile below the surface and temperatures regularly falling to minus 45°C, what attraction can this immense landscape possibly have as a tourist destination?

Those who have felt the attraction provide the answer. They describe it as a great privilege to step upon this awe-inspiring continent – a virgin paradise for wildlife, with incomparable scenery of mountains, snow and ice. Its unique magic has drawn explorers, adventurers and scientists for two centuries, and recently world travellers have been able to join them. Taking advantage of the long days of the austral summer, November through to March, visitors can observe vast colonies of penguins and pods of great whales, seals resting lazily on ice floes, storm petrels and wandering albatross with twelve-foot wing-spans. And always surrounded by magnificent vistas: icebergs in all their marvellous variety

of shape, size and colour; towering glaciers and dramatic cliffs that drop almost vertically into the sea, making everything in Antarctica appear larger than life.

Your hotel for this adventure is a special kind of ship – Quark Expeditions is the world's leading polar cruise expert, operating an adventure fleet of vessels to the Antarctic Peninsula area as well as powerful polar icebreakers which allow access to otherwise unreachable shores. Compared to the standards described elsewhere in this book, their vessels cannot be described as luxurious, but they do offer warm, comfortable accommodation for a lucky fifty to a hundred passengers. The small number of berths allows for easy access to shore, and enables an open-deck policy where passengers are welcome to visit the bridge at any time. This provides a fascinating place to watch ship operations and maintain a lookout for wildlife.

All cabins face seawards, with ensuite bathrooms and two berths. Some rooms open on to a promenade and most have circular

portholes or windows. Throughout the day the expedition leader communicates by way of a loudspeaker system piped into cabins for general announcements. In place of a newspaper, a daily itinerary is published each evening and distributed to cabins, listing lectures, meal hours and planned activities.

To make the most of the long hours on board, expedition staff – selected for their erudition as naturalists, historians, geologists and photographers – educate passengers with entertaining videos and slide-illustrated presentations. On-board amusements include a central VCR station in the hotel manager's office from which videos are piped into the suites, lounge and bar. In addition, the small library holds a selection of polar books, reference materials and general reading along with board games and playing cards.

Once you've gained your sea-legs, meals are served in a large open dining room (on dampened tablecloths to avoid sliding plates) during one informal sitting. Breakfast is

Port Lockroy. (opposite) **Exploring in a kayak.**

served buffet-style. At lunch and dinner a choice of Ocean (fish), Explorer (meat) or Antarctic (vegetarian) dishes is offered, featuring international cuisine. Throughout the day coffee and tea are available in the library, with mid-afternoon snacks and cakes. Service is very personal, with everyone mucking in – a combination of young international staff and experienced Russian crew. It's reassuring to know that the ship is crewed by a grizzled Russian captain and officers well experienced in ice operations and navigation under the severe conditions of the Russian Arctic.

Your adventure starts in Ushuaia, the world's southernmost city. Waving goodbye to its colourful buildings, you sail eastwards along the scenic Beagle Channel. Passing the legendary Cape Horn, you realise with some trepidation that while technology has progressed beyond recognition over the last century, Mother Nature has changed very little: the Drake Passage is as perilous as it ever was, and regularly lives up to its miserable reputation. Anything not screwed down is thrown around the cabin like something out of *Poltergeist*, while at every moment your eyes

search longingly for land. But all sea-sickness is forgotten with your first glorious glimpse of the silent shimmering towers of an iceberg the size of the Empire State Building drifting past. After crossing over the Antarctic convergence (a biological barrier where cold polar waters sink beneath the warmer waters of the more temperate zones) icebergs can, and do, appear at any time.

After forty-eight hours at sea, the expedition team are keen to grab the earliest opportunity to take weary passengers from ship to shore, but they are often thwarted when the temperature drops and the ocean surface freezes. As you travel along Iceberg Alley, the radar screen resembles the quantum level of a Nintendo game, requiring precise navigation through the maze of drifting bergs – officers are alert with eyes peeled, while passengers are hushed. When the captain has granted the all-clear, voyagers – garbed in Gortex, gumboots and life-jackets – are at last able to board the fleet of sturdy Zodiac craft and take their first steps on to Antarctica.

Once ashore, you may see dozens of adélie penguins waddling comically down the beach, followed by cacophonous chants as others

peer down at you from cliff escarpments. Down at the shoreline two giant grey-brown rocks look as though they're starting to move – enormous male elephant seals hump their blubbery mass over hoary basalt pebbles as penguins meander between them unperturbed. As you stare out across the icy Bransfield Strait, it's hard to believe that there are nine active volcanoes in the area.

If you're going to make the most of any landing opportunity, you have to be ready at any time of day or night – though during the Antarctic summer there are only two hours of darkness. As you step out of your cabin at four in the morning, the icy air makes itself felt. The long black pebble beach at Half Moon Bay is scattered with chinstrap penguins climbing the steep escarpment towards a wide ridge from where both sides of the island are visible, covered by thousands of pairs of nesting penguins. Walking is arduous – the snow, decorated with pinkie-brown penguin poo, is often thigh deep; and as each step creates a manmade penguin trap it has to be carefully infilled before continuing. Walkers are surrounded by the guano stench of implausible penguin motorways congested with dozens of

(opposite) **Hotel-cum-polar ice-breaker.** **Ice sculptures.**

murky brown chinstraps sliding down for their early morning swim. They pop out of the water and scramble off the ice on to the beach cleansed and pristine white again.

At Cuverville base camp, gentoo penguins chatter incessantly, sounding like the small cries of babies as they protect and incubate their eggs on their pebble nests. Further along the fjord passengers can disembark at Neko Harbour on to the peninsula itself. Active tidal waters are a continual threat here – thunderous cracks are followed by crashing walls of ice collapsing into the bay, causing a huge cascade of waves. Ascending to the ridge, the views are breathtaking and something of Antarctica's scale is embedded into your thoughts. Icebergs dwarf the ship, which looks like nature's plaything – a tiny rubber duck in an Olympic swimming pool. After the hard hike up, it's pure juvenile ecstasy to use the trodden path as a giant playground slide, and zoom back down on your bottom.

Passing Paradise Harbour, you may see minke whales gently crossing the bow as their distinctive fins dip in and out of the glassy waters. A water safari around the bay is a highlight for every traveller. Leopard seals unfazed by human activity gracefully drop into the water and dance around the Zodiacs. Slender icicles plucked from an overhang melt instantly in your mouth, tasting like nothing on earth, and

in the silence the world has never felt stiller, more serene or more beautiful.

Once you're back on board, staff have another treat up their sleeves – a barbecue. As crew and guests dance around the deck to Russian pop, others eat ribs and sausages, or cradle their steaming cups of spiced wine in gloved hands. You feel this end-of-the-world venue is hosting a party that the Great Gatsby himself would be in awe of.

The finale to the trip is a Zodiac expedition through the narrow Lemaire Channel, the motionless hushed waters flanked by soaring black basalt cliffs hundreds of metres high and covered in fresh snow. The ocean around Pléneau Island is so calm that it looks like a mirror, reflecting the images of the icebergs so perfectly that you could mistake the waters for land. Looking down through the turquoise surface to the infinities of black, the true size of these gargantuan floating islands can be appreciated – where no remains of broken huts or derelict walls signify man's transient visit to earth.

Around Port Lockroy, however, the English base has been preserved as a museum of what life was like for the inhabitants living and working there eighty years ago – it actually looks rather comfortable with sheepskin mattresses, good food stocks and a reliable Aga for warmth and cooking. As you post your

crown-stamped postcards in the red pillar-box you can whisper your quiet goodbye to Antarctica, with the explorer Ernest Shackleton's words in your heart:

We have seen God in his splendours,
Heard the text that nature renders,
We have reached the naked soul of man.

The Month

November is late spring in Antarctica, and is undoubtedly the most adventurous and in some ways the most awe-inspiring month to visit due to the unmelted mass of ice and snow. Wildlife attractions include incredible courtship displays in the penguin rookeries, with avaricious stone stealing and nest building; while isolated scientists in the research centres welcome the first visitors of the season.

The polar regions are cold even in summer – but probably not as cold as you'd imagine; the temperatures in the interior in November range from minus 15° to minus 45°C (5° to minus 49°F). Apart from global wind currents, Antarctica actually creates its own wind systems in which cold dense air slides from the high interior ice fields towards the lower areas along the coasts. At the edges of the ice plateau the winds accelerate, thereby lifting and blowing clouds of snow high into the air. Wrap up warm!

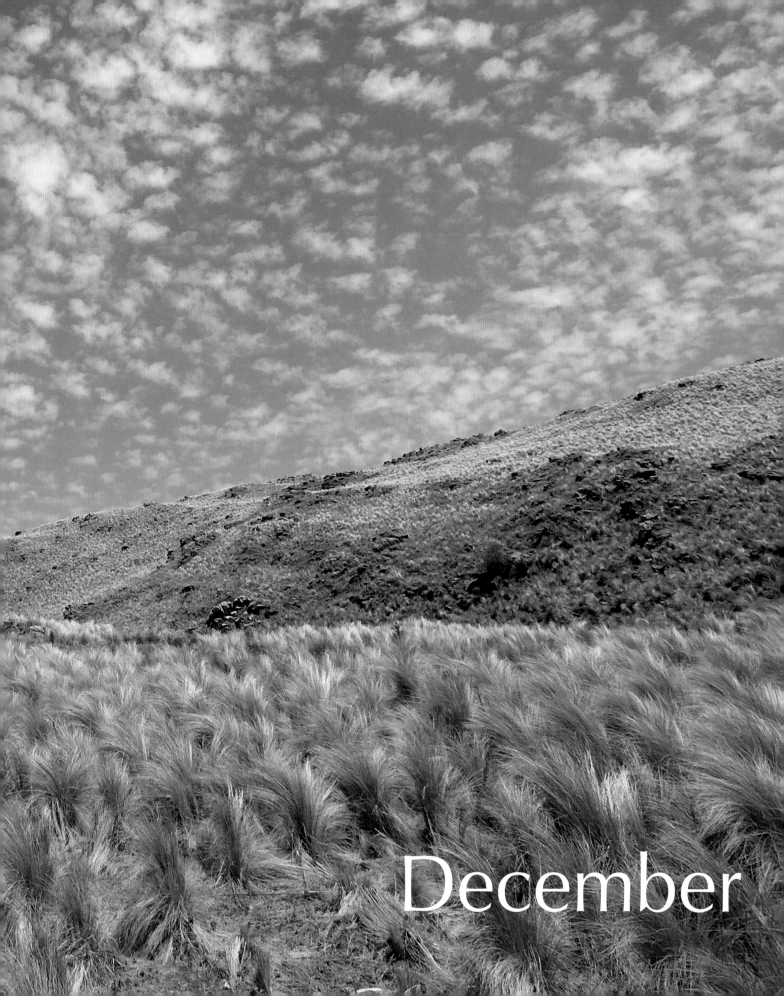

December

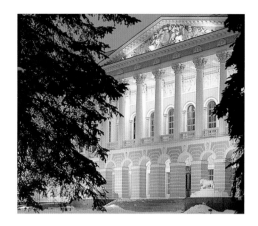

Grand Hotel Europe

St Petersburg

Branded as the northern capital of Russia, St Petersburg is also identified as the city of the Tsars and the Venice of the north. Situated in north-east Russia where the River Neva spills out onto the Gulf of Finland, it is known as the Land of Izhora – a gateway to the Baltic Sea connecting the east with the west.

Surprisingly, this cultural colossus laid its first cornerstone only 300 years ago, when Tsar Peter the Great realised that he needed powerful fortifications if he was to keep the Baltic coast trading route open following Russia's Northern War with Sweden. And so in 1703 the Peter and Paul Fortress was built on the marshes of Zayachy Island. The Tsar quickly drained the marshland, building a fine city based round a grand network of canals and elaborate palaces. Above the Admiralty Spire a golden ship was placed, crowning the city, and is recognised as St Petersburg's symbol to this day. In the twenty-first century it is a cultural treasure house, with over a thousand palaces and more than fifty museums including the magnificent Hermitage.

The uniform baroque façades lining the city's streets and canals hide lavish interiors and priceless art collected over centuries by Russian princes. The Grand Hotel Europe is one of these grand old dames, confident of her place in history and unassumingly present. Recognised as the city's best five-star hotel and premier meeting place, the 'Europe' as she is commonly referred to, is redolent of the charm of a bygone era. If not a hotel, this building would stand as a museum of Art Nouveau.

Located in the middle of the city's main and finest street, Nevsky Prospect, the Grand Hotel Europe is a landmark buffered by the Mikhailovsky Palace (also designed by the same architect), otherwise known as the Russian Museum, the Philharmonic Society and the unmistakable Church of the Resurrection.

The hotel's rich, varied past includes time served as an orphanage during the Bolshevik Revolution in 1917 at the height of the First World War. Originally built as a four-storey house in 1824 and added to by two more houses in 1825, the façade seen today was created in the 1830s by the famous Italian–Russian architect Carlo Rossi, who united the three properties. It was opened as the hotel 'Kuolon' and later renamed in 1872 as the 'Evropeyskaya Hotel', selling rooms from 1 to 30 silver roubles a night and vodka for 'first glass 1 rouble, second and following 20 kopecks only'!

The opening was proudly announced in the Stock Exchange newspaper and makes amusing reading for today's discerning traveller: '260 exclusively decorated rooms, restaurant, butcher shop, baker's, pastry shop, tailor, shoe repair, barber, fish smoking, wine cellars, 1–4 horse carriages for rent, laundry, ice producing room and lemonade production, interpreters with all the world's languages, furniture factory in the wing building for the hotel's needs, special lifting machines for our guests to all levels, telegraph… All the rooms are equipped with special modern air bells: to call for water, pull once, to call for a chambermaid pull the rope twice.'

(opposite) **L'Europe restaurant.**   **The imperial staircase.**

While today there are mini bars and telephones in every room for service, the hotel is strongly characterised by the Art Nouveau Jugend-style interiors, created between 1905 and 1914 by the Swedish-Russian architect Fyodor Lidvall. An appreciation for this period of living is certainly necessary to enjoy the austere furnishings that are rather Spartan by today's tastes.

After entering the discreet and somewhat modest entrance, turn left towards the main staircase, where the nostalgia really begins. The lobby bar's dark woods and twilight lighting emphasise the rays streaming through the Nouveau-style stained-glass

window behind the bar. You wouldn't be surprised to see a man in black leather, accompanied by a waif-like beauty dressed in top-to-toe fur, ordering a fat Cuban cigar and vodka, looking set for his next 007 mission.

The elegant imperial staircase, flanked with gilded cachepots holding aspidistras and carpeted in Russian red, leads to the Michelin-standard L'Europe restaurant. This area is the hotel's pièce de résistance – a living relic of modern Nouveau with magnificent stained-glass masterpieces framing the roof and each end of the room. Bright naked bulbs light the balcony alcoves and palm trees mingle with the tables. Each day a musician – be it harpist

at breakfast or trio at dinner – plays to diners from the elevated stage underneath the key-hole-shaped stained-glass window, while they savour the flavours of the finely prepared lobster, foie gras, quail or truffles.

The other restaurants include the intimate Caviar Bar, which features a long white marble bar and traditional Russian samovar. The Beluga is chilled on ice on a specially designed trolley and served with bliny or rosti, smetana, egg and finely sliced onion, and is guaranteed to be the best in St Petersburg. There is also an Italian restaurant, Rossi's, and a Chinese restaurant, Chopsticks, both offering fine fare. The bars include Sadko's, a popular

Black and white tiled bathroom. **Belle Chambre.** (opposite) **The Hermitage.**

cocktail bar – always filled with guests exchanging notes about the wonders of the Meriinksy Ballet, the Hermitage or Catherine's Palace – and an atrium coffee bar on the mezzanine close to the hotel shops selling souvenirs and famous Lomonosov porcelain.

The enormously dedicated general manager, Henri Belin, is most pleased with the impeccable standards of service he has managed to achieve here, unmatched anywhere in St Petersburg – reflecting his own excellence as a host. Plans are afoot to create Russia's first training school at the hotel, encouraging nationals to enter the industry and gain top-notch proficiency. Staff notably aim to please and work hard to exceed the expectations of all their guests: east is definitely meeting west.

The 301 bedrooms are distinguished by their inconspicuous red or black number placards; the red signify rooms furnished with original antiques, while the black are furnished with reproductions. In some instances it is difficult to tell the difference. The lofty ceilings, parquet floors, mahogany and damask- upholstered furniture are distinctively Nouveau and unlike any other

hotel room today. The characteristic black and white tiled bathrooms have also been renovated in their original Nouveau style. A particular favourite is room 135, the honeymoon suite – a modest 'belle chambre' (junior suite) prettily decorated with fine landscapes on the walls. Another striking room is 159, overlooking Nevsky Prospect's busy pavements.

Kings and queens, musicians, presidents, writers, actors, supermodels and global magnates continue to stay here each year and the visitors' book affirms this grand dame's unequalled status among its peers. Yesterday's footsteps included those of Tchaikovsky, H.G. Wells, Strauss, Stravinsky, Prokofiev, Pavlova and Chaplin; today it is Putin, Clinton, Harrison Ford, Prince Charles, Claudia Schiffer, Placido Domingo and Elton John who grace the marble corridors of the Grand Hotel Europe.

The Month

December sees St Petersburg covered in a mantle of snow, offering a Zhivago-like experience with deserted palaces, empty museums, troika rides through the parks of the tsars and steaming bowls of borscht.

Everyone but everyone wears a fur hat to keep warm in the minus 20°C temperatures as they wander the streets and canals marvelling at the 'white days' of winter. Previous hotel manager Elmar Greif has inaugurated a new cultural programme for the city between the months of November and March and named it 'White Days', during which special programmes have been collated combining the best opera, ballet and concert performances – without the queues.

During the hot summer months, tens of thousands of guests queue each day to enjoy the festivals of the 'White Nights' when the sun sets for only forty-five minutes. A huge cultural menu, including performances at the Meriinsky Theatre and the Hermitage and St Petersburg's palaces, churches and museums, attracts people from around the world. A popular destination for cruise liners, the streets can be hit with sudden surges as an already full city welcomes thousands more through its gates. A summer visit is essential if the fountains of Peterhof are the main attraction, otherwise leave it to the quieter months and have the delights of this beautiful city to yourself.

Eden Rock

St Barthélemy

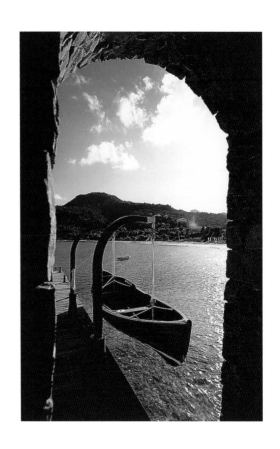

St Barth is the Caribbean's answer to St Tropez. People look chic, speak French and wear expensive perfumes; cars have French number plates and drive on the right; and bakeries smell of fresh croissants and *pain au chocolat*. It's so safe that there are practically no police and everyone knows everyone. Expression is *de rigueur* – a '*bouff*', '*ouff*' or *oo là là* with a raised eyebrow or a fleeting scowl says it all. You have to pinch yourself to remember you're not in Europe.

Compared to the verdant unspoilt pastures of St Kitts, or the mountainous peaks of St Lucia, St Barth's mainland is scraggy, scorched and uninviting, full of eroded rocks lined with holes – but its beaches and turquoise waters more than compensate. Known as the 'White Pearl of the Caribbean', it has no fewer than fourteen gleaming white sandy beaches. Its lack of drinking water was initially a bar to permanent settlement – in fact up until the twentieth century there was no source of fresh water anywhere on the island. Electricity only became available in

the 1960s and telephones were introduced some time in the 1970s.

Most people arrive by aeroplane, blissfully unaware that landing is a strategic knife-edge, plunging roller-coaster-style on to a narrow strip of concrete only 800 metres long. Miss it and you're in the sea – pilots receive special landing training and never get it wrong, I'm told.

Unlike most Caribbean islands, almost half the beds available to St Barth's visitors are in privately owned villas, cottages and apartments. There are a few small five-star hotels offering all the usual services, but most of the hotels are small family-run affairs. The local establishment realised that a disproportionate amount of development would bring long-term headaches, and consequently restricted the amount of building to practically nothing. A great decision and good news for tourism.

St Barth's most famous hotel, the Eden Rock, lies on a rocky promontory in the Bay of St Jean surrounded by a coral reef and beautiful turquoise waters with two white

sandy beaches unfurling from either side. A celebrated local adventurer, Rémy de Haenen, first built a house on stilts on the rock fifty years ago to entertain friends, including Greta Garbo who frequented it as her favourite hideaway. It has changed hands only once. David and Jane Matthews, an English couple, bought the house in 1995 intending to use it as a family holiday home. They inherited a small bar that they decided to keep running and, as often happens, one thing led to another – today the Eden Rock Hotel is one of Relais & Chateaux's most exclusive properties.

Jane has renovated each of the sixteen bedrooms according to its aspect on the rock, so that no two rooms are even vaguely similar. With a combination of European antiques and contemporary Caribbean furniture, four-poster beds, oil paintings and a kaleidoscope of silks and cottons from across the world, the result is an astonishing success. It's exciting opening each door knowing that the interior will be totally

Michael's Suite. (opposite) **Tapas on the rocks.**

different from the others and always decorated with impeccable taste.

Rooms vary from the cosy cabins ideal for young couples and teenagers to Caribbean cottages close to the sea with terraces, and rock-based suites with private balconies. Some bathrooms have showers carved out of the rock with seashell soap dishes and wonderful aromatherapy unguents. You can jump straight from your bed into the sea, and at night the rock is illuminated with underwater lights making it possible to watch fish and squid darting about as the quiet splash of waves rhythmically echoes around the rugged outcrop.

For the last seven years Jane's sister Pamela Parker has run the Eden Rock, and has succeeded in making St Barth's oldest hotel one of the best in the world. Most of the staff are French and the waiters are quick,

alert and efficient – not to mention chicly dressed in Ralph Lauren uniform.

St Barth is becoming increasingly renowned for its gourmet cuisine. At Eden Rock guests have a choice of three first-rate restaurants. At six foot six, Bordeaux chef Jean-Claude Dufour towers over all his staff. Having always lived by an ocean, his passion is cooking fresh fish and shellfood.

It was an ingenious idea to open a tapas restaurant. The On the Rocks Bar wraps around the rock and serves a varied selection of mouth-watering tapas on frosted square plates, including tuna sashimi with soya, crab spring rolls, grilled local shark and lobster ravioli, followed by sweet tapas such as chocolate custard with coffee sorbet or mango in a crisp with passion fruit sorbet.

Down on the beach the Sand Bar is strictly

shoeless and the perfect spot for delicious lunch time menus. A unique air-conditioning spray keeps you refreshed with eruptions of revitalising mist every fifteen minutes. It's a perfect spot to squander an hour or two out of the midday sun, and the fresh lobster is the best on the island.

Eden Rock's private open-air spa is an idyllic setting to benefit from a massage to the sound of the ocean as the sun sets. A fresh seawater pool has been carved from the rock overlooking the horizon – perfect for relaxation before or after the pampering. A new state-of-the-art spa is under development along the beach and will be ready by 2005.

Nearly all of St Barth's beaches are undeveloped, resulting in long stretches of wild private breezy shores with stunning

(opposite) **Steps to the sea.** **Rock restaurant.** **Harbour House suite.**

views, and anywhere on the island can be reached in less than half an hour. St Jean actually has two beaches divided by the Eden Rock promontory, where huge iguanas sprawl in their favourite sunspots. Green umbrellas and loungers covered in thick burgundy cushions line both beaches. Sailing, windsurfing, snorkelling, kayaking and deep sea fishing day trips to nearby islands are all available from the beach; other options, including scuba diving and crewed sailing charters, are also possible.

Although St Barth is a duty-free port with shopping opportunities ranging from a shaded table by the side of the road to chichi designer boutiques, it's definitely not the spot for champagne taste and beer money. The picturesque capital Gustavia is the main nucleus for shops including Cartier, Armani, Hermès and Ralph Lauren, with a few pretty boutiques along the road in St Jean.

Eden Rock has it all: the perfect Caribbean setting, French cuisine, classy British standards, style and design and an atmosphere all of its own. It's chic but certainly not stuffy and even the French, suppressing any thought of Gallic arrogance, find its fabulous geniality heartening.

The Month
St Barth's produces two varieties of weather: sunny bliss and hurricanes. Most of the year, puffy white clouds parade through a clear blue sky, and warm balmy breezes gently sway palm fronds only occasionally interrupted by a tropical shower.

From August to October, however, this halcyon state of affairs may be interrupted by a revolving tropical storm, which in its mature form turns into a hurricane. Locals joke that it's all the bad weather they've been spared during the rest of the year gathered together

into one package. By December any threat of hurricanes has past and the festive season is in full swing by Christmas – the perfect place to escape to for turkey à la plage. It's the time to see and be seen as the whole island becomes a party scene for people from across the world who consider St Barth their second home.

Estancia Los Potreros

Argentina

Way off the beaten track, on the top of the Sierras Chicas, nestled between the pampas and the Andes in the heart of the beautiful region of Córdoba, lies a paradise for people who love horses. Set in nearly 15,000 acres of secluded grassy wilderness, Estancia Los Potreros is an idyllic retreat for hikers and nature lovers. There's no sign to mark the turn-off on the rough earth road that snakes its way over the Sierras, and the odometers of some cars don't seem to coincide with the exact spot you're given.

Los Potreros is a working ranch, breeding Aberdeen Angus cattle and Paso Peruano pacing horses. It has remained in the same Anglo-Argentine family for four generations, and its origins go back to the establishment of Córdoba city in 1575. The estancia house dates from 1679, when the principal occupation was breeding mules for the silver mines in Peru – it was from this activity that the name Los Potreros, meaning 'enclosures for equines', derived. The present owner's grandfather became actively involved in

ranching for a different cause. He combed the area for mules, having to go as far as Bolivia to muster the large numbers needed for the Second World War, and sailed from Buenos Aires to India with 750 'healthy strong beasts' for the war effort.

The riding terrain is vast and varied, ranging from steep rocky paths down tree-studded gullies, to open, grassy hilltops and earthen roads. From the top of the oldest mountain range in South America you can see the city of Córdoba 50 kilometres away sitting in the pampas below; from the other side of the range you can see the Punilla Valley and the Sierras Grandes beyond.

The estancia is nestled below the brow of a hill, surrounded by acacia, coco and molle trees and a burst of wild flowers including red, white and purple verbena, and the magnificent magenta of glandularia. Underfoot – or crushed by a hoof – the intoxicating scents of peperina, wild mint, thyme and palo amarillo rise in the breeze. Separate from the house, the swimming

pool commands an excellent view of the surroundings and the activities on the farm.

The house is a traditional Córdoba farmhouse surrounding a large grass patio where Argentine *bochas* or bowls is often played. Mostly constructed of whitewashed adobe with square columns around the open patio, the dwelling is north-facing and its elevated position provides stunning views of the garden and hills beyond. The drawing room is formal but has a relaxed feel; sofas group round a stone fireplace, and antique ponchos, old family photos and paintings of favourite horses decorate the walls.

All seven bedrooms have wood-burning stoves, giving the place a very special atmosphere, and the comfortable antique beds and original Argentine coffers lend an authentic air. Each room has a private bathroom with both a bath and a shower, and fresh flowers from the meadows adorn side tables. Local rugs are on wooden floors, and walls are covered in paintings mostly of horses and local scenes. In attending to visitors,

Meals prepared with fresh farm produce.   'Ride like an Argentine'.

(opposite) **Chippendale furniture in a ranch setting.**

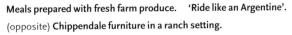

nothing is too much trouble for the family hosts or long-established staff, and the overall atmosphere is that of a house party.

Guests eat in the formal dining room, where the Chippendale furniture is complemented by fine English prints on the walls. A relaxed breakfast (if you haven't departed on an early ride) is usually taken on the stone patio under the bamboo pergola. Meals are varied and delicious with opportunities to try regional dishes. *Locro* is an eclectic dish and *empanadas* must be tried. The excellent cook makes the most delectable pastas and meat dishes, usually with produce from the farm. After a long day in the saddle, guests make an effort to dress, albeit informally, for dinner.

To accompany the dishes the local winery makes a delicious 'Los Potreros' wine, a Malbec and a Torrontes, so popular that the owner often jokes about forming a healthy subsidiary business. There are regular impromptu tastings of local wines for interested guests. Lunches can be sumptuous *asados*, Argentine barbecues, when endless cuts of meat are offered until the taker can accept no more. During a ride there are picnics with well-deserved drinks in the shade of weeping willows beside fast flowing crystal-clear streams.

English-educated Robin Begg and his wife Teleri run Los Potreros with the help of their three daughters and young son. They offer a unique combination of colonial-style estancia life with long-distance riding in one of Argentina's most beautiful landscapes.

Around the ranch you'll frequently happen upon friendly encounters with local people. Gaucho culture and reverence of the horse are never stronger than here, and brings with it the oldest traditions of Argentina. To 'ride like an Argentine' probably refers to stylish polo players, but the gaucho is at the root of this tradition and everywhere people appear stuck to their saddles at work or at play.

Those less interested in riding, or simply wanting a break, will enjoy just lying by the pool or walking in the hills and exploring the streams around the estancia. These wind their way down the hills, often forming small waterfalls and ponds that make refreshing stops for the ranch Labradors and baked hikers alike. Ornithologists are attracted by the huge variety of bird species, from soaring vultures and eagles to brightly coloured humming-birds. Condors have recently returned to the hills, and partridge and doves are plentiful throughout the year. Around the estancia foxes and hares are often seen, though the puma, wild boar and small deer are more elusive.

Culture and history lovers come to visit the Jesuit churches and interesting villages set throughout the captivating countryside, while golfers are gratified by the three good golf

(opposite) **Local gaucho.**   **Antique beds in lofty rooms.**

courses all within an hour's radius. Only one hour away is the unspoilt university city of Córdoba, the second largest in Argentina, once a principal staging post between Lima in Peru and Buenos Aires.

Most people come to ride with the gauchos – a sure way to get a true insight into rural life in Argentina. The horses, all bred on the estate, are handsome, well kept and docile, and the thick sheepskins over British army saddles make for a comfortable ride. There are plenty of opportunities for you to canter, although most of the riding is done at a fast walk if riders are using the ranch's superb string of Paso horses. The unique Peruano, pure descendants of the horses of the Conquistadors, can take you at canter speed while still walking – an unbelievable experience! There are also large, smooth-gaited Criollos crossbreeds and Peruano–Criollo crosses.

It is no surprise that the estancia is celebrated for its exceptional horses.

Riding is usually centred on estancia life, with occasional overnight excursions. Longer expeditions can easily be arranged to explore the vast area across the Sierras, when you could expect to be in the saddle between five to six hours a day. Nights away from Los Potreros are spent camping or in local dwellings, allowing visitors to experience another way of life, but most people opt for the shorter rides around the estate. Helping the gauchos is very popular – and those with extra energy can bring in the three milking cows!

The Month

Córdoba is known for its good weather and healthy climate: *siempre de temporada* ('always in season') is the old slogan. December is warm and the vegetation turns a lush, fresh green as the fruit literally drops from the trees. Apples, apricots, plums and, most anticipated of all, wild cherries, are plentiful and the smells spilling out from the kitchen promise a year of wonderful jam. The first rains have usually fallen and spring is well on its way. This is not the warmest month or the wettest, but the days can be very hot and the cool spring water in the swimming pool is a shocking and refreshing delight. When it does rain it usually thunders down and then clears back to blue skies with stargazing possible most nights.

For four days on either side of the full moon in December, there is an opportunity to take part in the 'full moon ride'. Horses can see at night and, with a full moon, so can humans. Saddlebags are stacked with refreshments for midnight feasts and riders head off on a great summer experience, not to be missed.

Kids

Easter Holidays

The Jumeirah Beach Hotel

Dubai

Once a small fishing port, the Gulf Coast emirate of Dubai is now a fascinating fusion of ancient culture and vibrant modernity. Its oil wealth has enabled it to invest in desalination plants, telecommunication systems and all the trappings of technology but, when the oil runs out, Dubai can fall back on one commodity that will never run out: the sun.

All-year sunshine has made this a popular choice for solar-starved Europeans. Add to this white sandy beaches, superb facilities and excellent service, plus great shopping, golf and racing, and it's easy to see why Dubai has been catapulted into the leading ranks of world-class holiday destinations. And to consolidate its position, Dubai is building the most ambitious leisure complex ever imagined: Palm Island, a huge, palm-tree-shaped archipelago of man-made constructions, standing proudly in cerulean waters.

Another stunning construction is a prominent wave of radiant blue glass known as the Jumeirah Beach Hotel, housing 600 sea-facing rooms, suites and villas on twenty-

six floors. It has unspoilt beaches, four swimming pools, a magnificent variety of restaurants and sporting facilities, and a terrific kids' club – in fact, of all the top hotels along this coastal strip, the Jumeirah offers the optimum experience for families: of course there are superb facilities for adults, but children are by no means sidelined.

Entering the hotel, you're immediately drawn into its 'Elements of Nature' theme. Different floors represent earth, air, fire and water through distinct colour schemes dividing the hotel into four separate levels: restful blues and greens for water; comforting browns and muted reds for earth; tranquil blues and white for air; and brilliant reds and yellows depicting a vibrant sun.

The theme of nature's elements is carried throughout the bedrooms and corridors, culminating in the Atrium, which features a colossal sculpture 90 metres high, portraying a satellite view of the earth with the United Arab Emirates at its centre, complete with a galaxy of stars and a moon in orbit.

Dining is a serious affair in Dubai and is at the heart of the Jumeirah Beach Hotel, whose twenty restaurants, cafes and bars represent every region of the world. The Apartment Restaurant is based on the concept of a 'home away from home' interior of a residential apartment, and includes a bar, music room, cellar and dining room offering a gourmet menu prepared by two-star Michelin chef Patrick Lenotre.

On the twenty-fifth floor, La Parrilla is the first and only Argentinean restaurant in the region, where fine steak is cooked before your eyes to a melting tenderness while tango musicians and dancers cavort around the room. Al Khayal is a traditional Lebanese restaurant styled after an Arabic tent. The Palm Court has all the ingredients for the perfect early, afternoon or late tea, or for pre- and post-dinner drinks, overlooking the lush gardens to the sounds of classical music. Der Keller reflects the atmosphere of a stylish, rustic German restaurant serving traditional food from different parts of Germany,

(opposite) **Sinbad's Kids' Club.**   **Wild Wadi Water Park.**

Switzerland and Austria, including wiener schnitzel, roesti and the well-known apfelstrudel. Alternatively, choose Carnevale – an authentic Italian restaurant offering traditional pastas.

If you take a trip along the Marina breakwater you reach one of Dubai's most ingenious venues – the circular Marina Seafood Market, elegantly decorated and offering the freshest and finest seafood in the Gulf, displayed on a specially designed ice show table. It's worth trying the innovative Asian fusion menu that combines traditional dishes from Asia with new European cuisine.

Situated on the ground floor of the Pavilion Marina, the Waterfront Restaurant allows easy access to the hotel's private beach and marina where children can enjoy time in the sand while parents are having lunch. The Dhow and Anchor doubles as a traditional British pub and a family restaurant; those who enjoy ales are well accommodated in the cosy pub area where seven draught beers are served. The restaurant has two dining areas, one inside and the other on the terrace area. The inside area is snug and reflects a typical pub style, while the stunning terrace descends over three levels and affords spectacular views of the pool, gardens, and the neighbouring hotel Burj Al Arab (the tallest in the world) – ideal for a casual teatime.

Between meals there are plenty of options for amusement. The Sports Club overlooking the beaches is a two-storey building situated on the Marina breakwater between the bay and tennis courts. Downstairs it offers many activities including tennis, squash, water sports and a PADI dive centre. Upstairs features a gymnasium with sixty nautilus machines and a free weights section. In addition, the health suite incorporates two saunas, three hot tubs, a steam room, Jacuzzi, plunge pool and two massage rooms offering aromatherapy, reflexology, shiatsu and facials. Throughout the day fitness classes are held, including yoga, karate, body pump and body combat.

Outside there are four swimming pools. The leisure pool features a walk-in Jacuzzi, chilled plunge pool and submerged airbeds as well as a swim-up pool bar located at the shallow end – but if you enjoy swimming lengths, the 25-metre training pool should prove good exercise. The family pool, surfaced in a sole-friendly material, has a walk-in 'beach' effect at one end and a rock wall incorporating a water slide at the other. Neighbouring the family pool is a shallow, shaded children's pool containing water play equipment, ideally located right next door to Sinbad's Kids' Club, which has a clubhouse designed like a ship.

The club offers a programme of activities for children aged between two and twelve

years, under the supervision of highly trained and qualified staff. Children can come and go throughout the day between 8 a.m. and 9 p.m. and take part in the daily activity programme, which includes arts and crafts, nature trails and swimming games.

Small children flock to the family adventure playground, consisting of raised walkways with a variety of safety-conscious padded play features including swings, tunnels and rope walkways. For older children the water sports on offer include sailing, water skiing, parasailing, snorkelling, wind surfing, scuba diving, kayaking, boogie boarding, wake boarding and banana boating.

For all guests, other outdoor facilities include seven floodlit competition standard tennis courts, one of which is multipurpose to include volleyball and basketball, a mini putting green and golf driving nets surrounded by three butler-serviced beaches.

Last but certainly not least, the next-door Wild Wadi Water Park is an attraction as popular with adults as it is with children. For guests of the hotel, entry is free to the twelve acres of themed water activities that includes twenty-three adrenaline-pumping rides that leave you gasping for more.

In a nutshell, the Jumeirah experience is a never-ending kaleidoscope – a fantastic fun factory in the sun for kids of all ages.

Ickworth

England

A short cry from Cambridge and the wild Suffolk coastline, close to the medieval town of Bury St Edmunds, a new concept for happy family holidays has emerged, where 'child friendly' no longer means that parents have to compromise on their creature comforts.

The present house at Ickworth was begun in 1795, the dream of the famously eccentric Fourth Earl of Bristol and Bishop of Derry. He enlisted an Italian architect who never even visited the site, to design the house.

Ickworth's extraordinary central rotunda and curving wings were intended to house the treasures the Earl Bishop collected from all over Europe – but his wife condemned it as a 'stupendous monument of folly'. Sadly, he didn't live long enough to see it completed and exhausted relatives finally gave up, leaving the west wing in shell form to this day.

Gifted to the National Trust in the 1950s, Ickworth remained the family seat of the Hervey family until 1999, when the colourful Seventh Marquis of Bristol died. It was with great vision and guts that Nigel Chapman and

Nicholas Dickinson eventually won the bid to renovate the east wing. It took three years of tireless work to bring it back to life and transform it into a unique, luxury, child-friendly hotel, accommodating up to thirty families.

The current owners decided early on not to recreate the interior according to the traditional layout used by the family for centuries. So the rooms no longer hark back to days long gone but are refreshingly contemporary. Style and comfort are uppermost in keeping with its grand stature, but the new policy makes everywhere sticky-finger friendly. Children are encouraged not to feel obliged to be on best behaviour, and can skip or sprint down the galleries without compunction.

Arriving is dramatic. The driveway leads through miles of open parkland up to the stepped main entrance of the house into the vaulted stone cloister on the ground floor. This is dominated by a billboard-size icon of a lady in a red ballgown – where you'll probably be greeted by tail-wagging Truffle, the hotel's black Labrador.

Within the hotel there are twenty-seven rooms, each named after a family member or a previous guest. Twenty-one of these are decorated in a semi-traditional style with chandeliers, deep window cushions and long silk drapes in rich tones of burgundy, topaz and turquoise. In addition there are six very contemporary rooms lit with spotlights and furnished with Molteni beds and King's Road designer fabrics. Whether you want to lord it in the Marquis's bedchamber or snuggle up in the butler's cosy retreat, the choices are equally comfortable. Children are allowed to stay for free when sharing their parents' room but there are also five interconnecting rooms if you'd rather enjoy your own space.

Bathrooms are hugely spacious and fabulously warm with piles of fluffy white towels and luxurious Aquae Sulis bath products.

In a secluded corner of the estate, 800 metres from the hotel, is the Dower House which contains a further eleven apartments ideal for large families or groups of friends. A specially converted dresser base with a

(opposite) **Classic bedroom.** **Luxury bathroom.** **Contemporary drawing room.**

convection/microwave oven, fridge and dishwasher enables you to make an easy meal or snack. To ease the carload, families with young children are provided with a cot, nappy bucket, changing mat, sterilisers, kettles and bottle warmers on request.

Manager Peter Lord, together with his wife Jane and their sons Christopher and William, are the perfect family hosts. Peter's desire to allow adults and children alike a sense of adventure and freedom is self-evident. As far as he is concerned, Ickworth is an escape from 'don'ts' and actively encourages plenty of 'do do dos'. Guests express their delight in the book of 'firsts' lying open on the hallway table. It is filled with joyful entries such as 'James and Daddy caught their first frog – it

survived', 'Daddy had his first facial', and an amusing 'the first and last time I will ever eat Roquefort ice-cream'.

All over the hotel you'll encounter friendly faces happy to stop and chat – the genuinely warm welcome and relaxing atmosphere enable every member of the family to chill out and feel totally at home.

The original cellar, known as 'The Street', is a huge passage connecting the east wing to the rotunda – so huge that in times gone by butlers had to speed along on bikes to keep the food warm on its way to the dining table. Now the cellar is home to the Four Bears' Den, a safe haven for babies and young children to play in while parents take a break. The Den is open each day from 10 a.m.

until 5 p.m, followed by high tea. It's stocked full of toys and art materials, and a daily list of activities is offered but certainly not forced. Children may be left for two-hour stints as many times as they wish during their stay; for older children, the semi-supervised Club Blu, complete with table football, table tennis and computer games, is an appealing option.

The old kitchens in the cellar are buzzing with life again too – as the Café Inferno – ideal for a quick homemade pizza for the children's supper while you enjoy caffè latte and biscotti. At the other end of the day, a full English breakfast is best taken in the light and spacious conservatory where kids can help themselves to pancakes and maple

Swimming Pool. **Adventures on the estate.** (opposite) **The long gallery.**

syrup, sausages, beans and cornflakes – all on one plate if they so desire!

Renowned for their lavish hospitality throughout the centuries, the Herveys entertained in style and the former family dining rooms continue to serve fine menus. After the children have gone to bed, treat yourself to a meal in Frederick's. A sophisticated baby-listening system operated from reception means you don't have to go running up to check every five minutes, and the food is as good as in any London dining club.

Back in that enormous cellar, there's also room for the Aquae Sulis Spa, inspired by the thermal mineral waters in Bath. The Spa offers a menu of therapeutic treatments for tired mothers and fathers looking for a little relaxation and pampering. The three treatment rooms are popular venues and managed by helpful therapists suggesting you opt for a 'slave to your skin' facial coupled with a shoulder and arm massage, 'handsome hands' men's manicure or 'TLC for Mums to be' – which includes an appropriately named 'can't reach your feet' treat.

One of the main attractions of the Ickworth estate is the extensive 1,800 acres of wooded parkland, created in part by Capability Brown – a living landscape rich in native plant and animal life. While some parts have been cultivated and grazed; most of the glorious English parkland can be explored and enjoyed on foot or by bicycle.

Surrounding the hotel are formal gardens created in the early nineteenth century by the First Marquis of Bristol. Beyond the church are the remains of an eighteenth-century garden created by the First Earl, and the original summerhouse and canal still survive. The kitchen garden, protected by a high brick wall, is today a vineyard producing Ickworth wines.

Outside the conservatory children are bemused to see a three-metre-high giraffe named 'Kilimanjaro' and three flamingos made from old motorbike parts.

Ickworth has something for everybody – a stunning house with a fascinating history and exquisite collections, an excellent restaurant, superb spa, plus professional and accommodating child-care. You'll also find enchanting

gardens, woodland walks, a family cycle route, jogging trail, adventure playground area, riding, plant centre and a well-stocked shop for mementoes. With all its facilities, it's an ideal retreat for children and adults of any age, epitomising great style without standing on ceremony. Adventure abounds if you have the yen for it.

Christmas Holidays

Evason Hua Hin

Thailand

Hua Hin is unlike most other beach resorts in Thailand: far from Bangkok's bright lights and frantic all-night action, it's very much a family holiday destination. As a seaside town, it offers the best Thai seafood in the country, served by so many international restaurants that you're spoilt for choice. On top of this, there's tempting shopping, nightly street markets and Thailand's first golf course.

It became popular as a summer retreat in the 1920s after the construction of the railway line from Bangkok. A beautiful colonial-style railway hotel was built near Hua Hin's famous rocks in 1923, and the area finally became well established as a beach resort when King Rama VII built a beachside palace named 'Klai Kangwon' where the Thai royal family customarily holiday each year.

Three hours south of Bangkok at Pranburi, roughly thirty kilometres south of Hua Hin, you'll find the Evason Hua Hin Resort and Spa. Set among twenty acres of beautifully landscaped tropical gardens filled with lotus ponds and waterways, the resort faces the Gulf of Siam. Designed and operated by Six Senses hotel guru Sonu Shivdasani (of Soneva fame), together with his creative director wife Eva, the hotel was bound to be a success from the outset. Jointly, they have moved away from using all too common old-fashioned stereotypical concepts and have created a mode of what Sonu describes as 'intelligent luxury'. This embraces a 'can do' style and service ethic that is a pleasure for guests and considerate to the local environment and indigenous population.

Eight separate two-storey buildings set among manicured tropical gardens accommodate 145 luxurious guestrooms. There are also forty generous stand-alone villas each with a private pool. A number of interconnecting Evason and Studio rooms have been designed with families in mind and are filled with child-friendly furniture, a box full of toys and various board games for hours of entertainment (a Sony PlayStation is also available on request, but this facility is considerately not broadcast).

All rooms have twin or king-sized beds covered in 'tropical tog' duvets, and a full-sized day bed that can be used as a sofa during the day. A third bed is available at night on request. Secluded pool villas, shaded by massive banana plants and coconut-laden palm trees, have the added benefits of their own butler, a private plunge pool and a sunken outdoor bathtub surrounded by a lotus pond – bath time has never been more popular! Fun is at the fore-front of every mind, and at night housekeepers place sand-filled cotton lizards under pillows and bed legs to amuse children.

High-quality dining at affordable prices is a major consideration at Evason, with a number of gourmet options for all tastes. The Restaurant serves a sumptuous buffet breakfast including popular local dishes in a semi al fresco location, to the sound of local musicians playing *kaens*, *suengs* and *ranardaiks*.

The casual open-air Beach Restaurant next to the seashore entertains children with its windowed show kitchen operating a traditional wood-fired pizza oven. It serves

'Intelligent luxury' in the bedroom.　(opposite) **The Restaurant.**

gourmet breakfasts to the sound of the ocean's waves, an à la carte lunch menu, and a special seafood menu at dinner that changes daily. Beside the pool a two-level open-air bar offers a sophisticated snack menu – ideal for kids' lunches at any time of day – and a special gourmet dinner menu.

At night the whole hotel is transformed by hundreds of flickering candles illuminating paths throughout the grounds, lending an atmosphere of sanctuary and calm after a full day with the children. The Other Restaurant specialises in creative Asian fusion cuisine, and opens for dinner in either the chic air-conditioned dining room or al fresco courtyard for those who prefer to dine in the balmy tropical air overlooking terraced lotus ponds.

Evason's holistic Six Senses spa is one of the prettiest in Asia, and provides an extensive menu of relaxing and revitalising treatments in the five thatched *salas* each surrounded by tranquil pools. Inside the spa, there are six treatment rooms, including three especially designed for couples, two dry saunas and

two steam rooms – it's definitely a place for expert pampering.

Facilities for children are exceptionally good. Younger ones are supervised by qualified staff dedicated to providing an exciting list of locally orientated activities including umbrella painting, Thai language lessons, kite flying, beach nature walks, batik printing, junior yoga, soap carving and archery, to name but a few. They're treated like little VIPs at 'Just Kids!' – the hotel's professionally managed club. Next to the Mr McGregor-style vegetable garden, the club has a canopied swimming pool with bamboo waterspout, adventure playground and huge activity list ideal for children aged between four and twelve. Real thought has gone into what children will enjoy and, while they're happy just to splash in and out of the pool most of the day, an hour or two of respite in the club is a welcome option for all parties.

Older children are offered such entertainments as elephant trekking, go-karting, tennis and swimming lessons. They can also enjoy the option of a sleepover – pitching their own

tents, setting up sleeping bags and roasting marshmallows on the bonfire while singing *Ging-gang-goolie* under the starlit sky.

It's easy to keep little girls out of the midday sun here. Down on the beach local Thai women cheerfully plait hair and paint nails under their shady canopies during siesta time. Throughout the day, staff walk around the poolside offering fresh water melon and ice lollies for 'good children' – and adults.

Adults in search of adventure can choose from a lengthy list of unusual activities including tandem skydiving, a workout around Thanarat's military camp, cave trekking, golf or leisurely sunset cruises.

Evason is an absolute hit for children and adults alike, meeting the needs of both in equal doses. Adults feel neither short-changed by the world-class standards of accommodation, food and spa facilities, nor uncomfortable having their little darlings running around barefoot in lolly-stained clothes chasing lizards. The only problem is that at the end of your stay your children will be utterly reluctant to leave – and so will you.

Directory *where to go*

Prices are included only as a guide and exclude any tax or meal plan details and are subject to change at any time.

January

Mount Nelson Hotel Cape Town
Mount Nelson Hotel, 76 Orange Street
Cape Town 8001, South Africa
TEL (00 27) 21 483 1000
FAX (00 27) 21 423 1060
WEB mountnelsonhotel.orient-express.com
Single Rooms from R 4660
Double Rooms from R 4790

The Datai Malaysia
The Datai, Jalan Teluk Datai, 07000 Pulau
Langkawi, Kedah Darul Aman, Malaysia
TEL (00 604) 9592500
FAX (00 604) 9592600
WEB www.ghmhotels.com
Rooms from RM 1,490

Tanjung Rhu Malaysia
Tanjung Rhu, Mukim Ayer Hangat, 07000
Pulau Langkawi, Kedah Darulaman, Malaysia
TEL (00 604) 959 1033
FAX (00 604) 959 1899
WEB www.tanjungrhu.com.my
Damai Rooms from RM 880

Villa Nova Barbados
Villa Nova, St John, Barbados, West Indies
TEL (00 1) 246 433 1524
FAX (00 1) 246 433 6363
WEB www.villanovabarbados.com
Deluxe Terrace Rooms from US$650
Children under the age of 12 are accepted
on a request basis.

February

Copacabana Palace Rio de Janeiro
Copacabana Palace, Avenida Atlântica 1702
Rio de Janeiro, CEP 22021-001, Brazil
TEL (00 55) 21 548 7070
FAX (00 55) 21 235 7330
WEB copacabanapalace.orient-express.com
Rooms from US$330
Suites from US$600

Pousada Marquesa Brazil
Pousada Marquesa, 99 Rua Dona Geralda
CEP 23970 – 000, Paraty, RJ, Brazil
TEL (00 55) 24 3371 1263
FAX (00 55) 24 3371 1299
WEB www.pousadamarquesa.com.br
Suites from BR 177
Annexe Rooms from BR 83

Ladera St Lucia
Ladera, PO Box 225, Soufrière
St Lucia, West Indies
TEL (00 1 758) 459 7323
FAX (00 1 758) 459 5156
WEB www.ladera-stlucia.com
One-bedroom Suites with plunge pool
from US$240

March

Four Seasons New York
Four Seasons Hotel, 57 East 57 Street
New York, New York 10022, USA
TEL (00 1) 212 758 5700
FAX (00 1) 212 758 5711
WEB www.fourseasons.com
Rooms from US$595.
Suites from US$1,350.

Chalet Eugenia Klosters, Switzerland
Chalet Eugenia, Talstrasse 83
7250 Klosters, Switzerland
To book, contact Descent International
Riverbank House, Putney Bridge
London SW6 3JD
TEL (00 44) 20 7384 3854
FAX (00 44) 20 7384 3864
WEB www.descent.co.uk
One week in Chalet Eugenia
from £15,995 for up to 12 guests

Rawlins Plantation Inn St Kitts
Rawlins Plantation Inn, PO Box 340
St Kitts, West Indies
TEL (00 869) 465 6221
FAX (00 869) 465 4954
WEB www.rawlinsplantation.com
Single Rooms from US$220
Double Rooms from US$310
The hotel is closed during August and September.
Children over the age of 12 are welcome.

April

Blakes Amsterdam
Blakes, Keizersgracht 384, 1016
Amsterdam, The Netherlands
TEL (00 31) 20 530 2010
FAX (00 31) 20 530 2030
WEB www.blakesamsterdam.com
Single Rooms from 250 Euros
Double Rooms from 390 Euros

Ashford Castle Ireland
Ashford Castle, Cong, Co. Mayo, Ireland
TEL (00 353) 9495 46003
FAX (00 353) 9495 46260
WEB www.ashford.ie
Standard Rooms from 291 Euros.
Lake-view Rooms from 335 Euros.
Suites from 730 Euros.
Jacket and tie are required dress
for gentlemen after 7 p.m.

Dhoni Mighili Maldives
Dhoni Mighili, North Ari Atoll
PO Box 2017, Republic of Maldives
TEL (00 960) 450 751
FAX (00 960) 450 727
WEB www. dhonimighili.com
Luxury dhoni with beach bungalow
and plunge pool from US$700.

.

May

Amanjena Marrakech
Amanjena, Route de Ouarzazate
KM 12, Marrakech, Morocco 40000
TEL (00 212) 44 40 33 53
FAX (00 212) 44 40 34 77
WEB www.amanresorts.com
Pavilion Suites from US$850
Two-bedroom Maison Suites from US$1,900

Hacienda de San Rafael Spain
Hacienda de San Rafael, Apartado 28
Carretera Nacional IV (KM 594), 41730
Las Cabezas de San Juan (Seville), Spain
TEL (00 95) 587 2193
FAX (00 95) 587 2201
WEB www.haciendadesanrafael.com
Courtyard Rooms 210 Euros.
Casitas 480 Euros.
The hacienda is open each year
from April to October.

Ananda India
Ananda, The Palace Estate, Narendra Nagar
Tehri-Garhwal, Uttaranchal – 249175, India
TEL (00 91) 1378 227500
FAX (00 91) 1378 227550
WEB www.anandaspa.com
Deluxe palace-view Rooms
US$300 single or US$330 double.
Deluxe valley-view Rooms
US$350 single or US$380 double

June

Hotel Ritz Madrid
Hotel Ritz, Plaza de la Lealtad 5
28014 Madrid, Spain
TEL (00 34) 91 701 6767
FAX (00 34) 91 701 6776
Orient-Express Hotels reservations:
020 8604 2242
WEB www.orient-express.com
Rooms from 480 Euros
Suites from 2,100 Euros

Hotel Eisenhut Germany
Hotel Eisenhut, Hergasse 3-7, D-91541
Rothenburg ob der Tauber, Germany
TEL (00 49) (0) 9861 7050
FAX (00 49) (0) 9861 70545
WEB www.eisenhut.com
Single Rooms from 111 Euros
Double Rooms from 155 Euros
Suites from 280 Euros.

Bovey Castle England
Bovey Castle, North Bovey, Dartmoor
National Park, Devon TQ13 8RE
TEL (00 44) 1647 445 000
FAX (00 44) 1647 440961
WEB www.boveycastle.com
Mews Rooms from £145
Garden View Rooms from £160
Valley View Rooms from £190
Deluxe Valley Rooms from £240
Suites from £450

July

George V Paris
Four Seasons Hotel George V
31 Avenue George V, 75008 Paris, France
TEL (00 33) 1 49 52 70 00
FAX (00 33) 1 49 52 70 10
WEB www.fourseasons.com
Superior Rooms from 680 Euros.
Suites from 1250 Euros.

La Bastide de Marie France
La Bastide de Marie, Route de Bonnieux
Quartier de la Verrerie, 84560 Ménerbe
France
TEL (00 33) 4 90 72 30 20
FAX (00 33) 4 90 72 54 20
WEB www.c-h-m.com
Rooms from 390 to 490 Euros.
Suites from 600 to 690 Euros.

Orient Express Safaris Botswana
Orient Express Safaris Botswana
PO Box 786432, Sandtown 2146
South Africa
TEL (00 27) 11 481 6052
FAX (00 27) 11 481 6065
WEB www.orient-express-safaris.com
Daily inclusive charge from US$654

August

Claridges London
Claridge's, Brook Street, Mayfair
London W1A 2JQ
TEL (00 44) 207 629 8860
FAX (00 44) 207 499 2210
WEB www.savoy-group.co.uk
Rooms from £315
Suites from £515

Skibo Castle Scotland
Skibo Castle, Dornoch, Sutherland
IV25 3RQ, Scotland
TEL (00 44) 1862 894600
FAX (00 44) 1862 894601
WEB www.carnegieclub.co.uk
Daily residential charge: £650-£800

Chateau Lake Louise Canada
The Fairmont Chateau Lake Louise
Lake Louise, Alberta, Canada T0L 1E0
TEL (00 1) 403 522 1803
FAX (00 1) 403 522 3111
WEB www.fairmont.com
Fairmont Rooms from US$260.

September

Palazzo Vendramin Venice
Palazzo Vendramin at the Hotel Cipriani
Guidecca 10, 30133 Venice, Italy
TEL (00 39) 41 520 7744
FAX (00 39) 41 520 3930
WEB www.orient-express.com
Vendramin Junior Suites from 1,200 Euros
The Cipriani is open from March to November
each year.
The Palazzo Vendramin and Palazzetto close
for a short time in January.

Oberoi Lombok
Oberoi Hotel, Medana Beach, Tanjung
PO Box 1096, Mataram 83001
West Lombok, NTB
TEL (00 62) 370 63 8444
FAX (00 62) 370 63 2496
WEB www.oberoihotels.com
Luxury Lanai Pavilion Rooms with garden view
from US$190.
Luxury villa from US$355.

King Pacific Lodge Canada
King Pacific Lodge, Princess Royal Island
British Columbia, Canada
TEL (00 888) 592 5464
WEB www.kingpacificlodge.com
3-night Friday to Monday Lodge Package
from US$2,590.
4-night Monday to Friday Lodge Package
from US$3,250.
Open from May to September each year.

October

Çırağan Palace Istanbul
Çırağan Palace Hotel Kempinski, Istanbul
Çırağan Caddesi No: 32 Besiktas, 34349
Istanbul, Turkey
TEL (00 90) 212 258 3377
FAX (00 90) 212 259 6687
WEB www.ciragan-palace.com
Park-View Rooms from US$384.
Bosphorus Rooms from US$520.
Palace suites from US$1,020.

The Oberoi Amarvilās Agra
The Oberoi Amarvilās, Taj East gate
Agra – 282 001, India
TEL (00 91) 562 223 1515
FAX (00 91) 562 223 1516
WEB www.oberoihotels.com
Deluxe Rooms from US$425

The Oberoi Vanyavilās Ranthambhore
The Oberoi Vanyavilās, Maarfarm
Ranthambhore Road, Sawai, Madhopur
Rajasthan – 322 001, India
TEL (00 91) 7462 223 999
FAX (00 91) 7462 223 988
WEB www.oberoihotels.com
Deluxe Rooms from US$475

The Oberoi Rajvilās Jaipur
The Oberoi Rajvilās, Goner Road
Jaipur, Rajasthan – 303 012, India
TEL (00 91) 141 268 0101
FAX (00 91) 141 268 0202
WEB www.oberoihotels.com
Deluxe Rooms from US$395
Luxury tent from US$475
Villa with pool from US$1500

The Oberoi Udaivilās Udaipur
The Oberoi Udaivilās, Haridasji Ki Magri
Udaipur, Rajasthan 313 001, India
TEL (00 91) 294 43 3300
FAX (00 91) 294 43 3200
WEB www.oberoihotels.com
Deluxe Rooms from US$395
Deluxe Rooms with terrace pool from US$475

Sharrow Bay England
Sharrow Bay, Lake Ullswater
Penrith, Cumbria, CA10 2LZ
TEL (00 44) 17684 86301
FAX (00 44) 17684 86349
WEB www.sharrow-bay.com
Rooms from £160.
Suites from £220.

November

Alvear Palace Buenos Aires
Alvear Palace Hotel, Av. Alvear 1891
(C1129AAA) Buenos Aires, Argentina
TEL (00 54) 11 4808 2100
FAX (00 54) 11 4804 9246
WEB www.alvearpalace.com
Palace Rooms from US$410.
Junior Suite from US$472.

explora en Atacama Chile
explora en Atacama, Hotel de Larache, Ayllú
de Larache, San Pedro de Atacama, Chile
TEL (00 56) 2 206 6060
FAX (00 56) 2 228 4655
WEB www.explora.com
Residential charge per person
from US$1,296 for three days

Quark Expeditions Antarctica
Quark Expeditions, Inc. 1019 Post Road
Darien, CT 06820, USA
TEL (00 1) 203 656 0499
FAX (00 1) 203 655 6623
WEB www.quarkexpeditions.com
11 day cruise from US$3,695

December

Grand Hotel Europe St Petersburg
Grand Hotel Europe, Mikhailovskaya Ulitsa
1/7, 191011 St Petersburg, Russia
TEL (00 7) 812 329 6001
FAX (00 7) 812 329 6005
WEB www.grandhoteleurope.com
Rooms from US$350
Junior Suites from US$460
Suites from US$750

Eden Rock St Barth
Eden Rock, St Jean Bay, 97133 St-Barthélemy
French West Indies
TEL (00 590) 5 90 29 79 99
FAX (00 590) 5 90 27 88 37
WEB www.edenrockhotel.com
Cottages from 475 Euros
Deluxe Rooms from 590 Euros
Suites from 760 Euros

Estancia Los Potreros Argentina
Estancia Los Potreros, Camino del Cuadrado
Sierras Chicas, Córdoba, Argentina
TEL & FAX (00 54) 3548 45 2121
WEB www.ride-americas.com
Daily all-inclusive charge £140 per person.

Kids

Jumeirah Beach Hotel Dubai
The Jumeirah Beach Hotel
PO Box 11416, Dubai, UAE
TEL (00 971) 4 3480000
FAX (00 971) 4 3482273
WEB www.jumeirahinternational.com
Rooms from 1350 UAE Dirhams
Two children below the age of twelve are free
when sharing their parents room.

Evason, Hua Hin Thailand
The Evason Hua Hin Resort and Spa
9 Parknampran Beach, Prachuab Khiri Khan
77220, Thailand
TEL (00 66) 32 632 111;
FAX (00 66) 32 632 112
WEB www.six-senses.com
Evason Rooms from 3,900 Thai Baht
Evason pool villa from 10,630 Thai Baht.

Ickworth England
The Ickworth Hotel, Horringer
Bury St Edmunds, Suffolk IP29 5QE
TEL (00 44) 1284 735350
FAX (00 44) 1284 736300
WEB www.ickworthhotel.com
Standard Double Rooms from £155.
Deluxe Doubles from £235.
Suites from £370.
Interconnecting Rooms from £400.
Children sleep for free when sharing their
parents' room.